WORLD WAR II
FROM ORIGINAL SOURCES

THE BATTLE
OF BRITAIN

EDITED BY BOB CARRUTHERS

Pen & Sword
AVIATION

This edition published in 2013 by
Pen & Sword Aviation
An imprint of
Pen & Sword Books Ltd
47 Church Street
Barnsley
South Yorkshire
S70 2AS

First published in Great Britain in 2012 in digital format by
Coda Books Ltd.

Copyright © Coda Books Ltd, 2012
Published under licence by Pen & Sword Books Ltd.

ISBN 978 1 78159 216 8

Printed and bound by CPI Group (UK) Ltd, Croydon, CR0 4YY

Pen & Sword Books Ltd incorporates the Imprints of Pen & Sword Aviation, Pen & Sword
Family History, Pen & Sword Maritime, Pen & Sword Military, Pen & Sword Discovery, Pen
& Sword Politics, Pen & Sword Atlas, Pen & Sword Archaeology, Wharncliffe Local History,
Wharncliffe True Crime, Wharncliffe Transport, Pen & Sword Select, Pen & Sword Military
Classics, Leo Cooper, The Praetorian Press, Claymore Press, Remember When, Seaforth
Publishing and Frontline Publishing

For a complete list of Pen & Sword titles please contact
PEN & SWORD BOOKS LIMITED
47 Church Street, Barnsley, South Yorkshire, S70 2AS, England
E-mail: enquiries@pen-and-sword.co.uk
Website: www.pen-and-sword.co.uk0

CONTENTS

THE BATTLE OF BRITAIN BEGINS: DEFENDING THE AIRFIELDS

W HEN A heavy AA gunfire's at night there is a Hash of flame 25 feet high, and there had never been a published picture of this instant. So it was arranged that an expert Press photographer should take one. Many have been taken since, but this was the first. He went to a gun site guarding Avonmouth and Bristol, which at the time (July 1940) were getting plenty of enemy attention. He focused his camera in daylight, got the four guns in the view-finder and fixed the tripod in position; he arranged to open his shutter when the gun position officer gave the command "Fuse!" and then settled down to wait.

The photographer, congratulated by an officer on a wonderful picture, moaned in reply that he hadn't got a picture at all. He was very depressed: he phoned his office and they told him to come home. Just to round off the story, he had to smash up his car on the way back to avoid a suicidal swerving cyclist.

Of course the story had a happy ending, for when, in a mood of self-torturing determination to pursue this fiasco to its final disappointment, he developed the pictures, there emerged the triumphant photograph in all that he could have ever wanted.

The Germans started the Battle of Britain with attacks on convoys, and then went on to harbours and dockyards. They bombed Chatham Dockyard. They delivered mass attacks on Portsmouth and Dover; they bombed Portland and Weymouth; and then, while still maintaining attacks on coastal towns, started a carefully-planned series of assaults against airfields.

The importance of AA guns in airfield defence is fundamental. It is the guns which guard the 'planes during the vital moments when they are getting off the ground. Wherever in this war airfields have lacked adequate AA defences, they have been unable to stay in action under any sustained attack. This was amply demonstrated in France and Crete. Nine of the airfields in South and South-east England came in for a battering, some of them twice on one day, and in a few instances airfields were attacked several times during a day.

Here is an example of the quick action and readiness of the anti-aircraft defence on airfields. One afternoon, when a number of our own aircraft were refuelling at a southern airfield, enemy raiders came and had an excellent chance of attacking the personnel and 'planes on the ground. The AA guns opened up at the raiders at once, with such success that the enemy could not get in to bomb or machine-gun the ground in spite of determined effort. They jinked and turned to starboard, and unloaded their bombs on a building at the side which had been a hospital, a small part of which was occupied as a military office. The airfield and the 'planes were saved by AA fire on that occasion, though the building which received the bombs was set on fire and partially destroyed.

On August 15th, Manston and Hawkinge airfields were dive-bombed by a hundred enemy aircraft which dived out of the sun with engines shut off. The raid split and 50 raiders attacked each place. In the Hawkinge attack a hangar was hit and some damage done to administrative buildings, but the landing ground was not affected. The formations were quickly broken by hot AA fire, and the enemy became so anxious to leave the area that his bombers threw away their bombs over Ramsgate and Broadstairs where private property and small civilian homes suffered. Some people were killed but no military casualties or damage resulted. Similarly at Manston airfield the landing ground was untouched: some damage, however, was done to surrounding building.

The next day Tangmere was attacked by 200 Junkers 87s. Then 24 Stukas, flying at 15,000 feet, dived in pairs to 1,200 feet. One of the Bofors brought a 'plane down with only two rounds, the first of which was a direct hit. This gun was firing over open sights. This was Tangmere's most serious raid. Seven R.A.F. personnel and two civilians were killed. But 20 enemy aircraft were brought down and the airfield was in action again within a few hours.

Three days later came another big-scale airfield attack. Kenley and Biggin Hill were among the main targets, and were attacked by raiders numbering 35 to 100 aircraft. Much damage was done. The attack on Kenley was made in two waves. The first was a low-level attack at 1.22 p.m. by nine Dornier 17s, flying as low as 50 feet. These raiders were plotted in the whole way from Newhaven. The searchlight control officer at Kenley said, "We followed the 'planes every inch of their journey, and knew they were making for us." The first three of the low-flying raiders machine-gunned the pits of the 3-inch guns manned by a Light AA Regiment and dropped bombs on the northern edge of the airfield. The remaining six raiders dropped high explosives and incendiaries on the Troop H.Q., the Hospital and the Hangars, scoring direct hits. In all 50 or 60 H.E. bombs were dropped.

A Messerschmitt 109 shot down by Lewis-gun fire in a Kent cornfield.

The high-level attack came from the direction of Dungeness and caused very little damage.

During their action against the raiders one of the 3-inch guns hit a Dornier square on the nose and brought it down. A gunner, who was knocked off his perch and wounded by bomb splinters, refused to leave his post. Some of the bombs were dropped from so low a level that they reached the ground still horizontal, and skidded along making grooves before they hit the wall of the Officers' Mess. All the R.A.F. telephone lines were wrecked; but fortunately the Army Lines to the Searchlight Batteries were unharmed, and over these medical aid was summoned. Lewis Gunners of the L.A.A. Regiment reported that their bullets seemed to glance off the enemy aircraft without having any effect. This was confirmed by the R.A.F. fighters, and was one of the first indications that the *Luftwaffe* were putting heavier armour on their machines. Nevertheless, twenty-nine enemy aircraft were brought down.

At Biggin Hill the story is similar. One hundred 'planes raided Biggin and 200 bombs were dropped. The Heavy and Light guns were in action, the former claiming one Dornier 215. The Bofors No. 2 gun site had a narrow escape. Three anti-personnel bombs were dropped in their compound, two of them missing the magazine only by inches. Splinters from one of these bombs killed the detachment cook, seriously wounded the Troop Commander and slightly wounded one other rank. Skilful plotting by a neighbouring Searchlight Battery saved many aircraft from being destroyed. Their preliminary reports enabled all aircraft, including even trainers, to be got off the ground in time. Finally, the operations room had to be evacuated. The Searchlight Control Officer went back to see that everything was clear and found that the one telephone left intact was ringing. It was a call from the Observer Corps. A voice asked, "Are you interested in a crashed Hurricane?" Bdr. E. W. Lelliott was praised for his cool leadership and the valuable notes which he took of new tactics used by the enemy 'planes.

The next day, August 19th, raiders were engaged by AA guns over the Thames Estuary. About 20 bombers with a large fighter escort appeared at 15,000 feet. The first 'plane to be hit by AA fire lost height rapidly and dived away to the south-east, eventually crashing near Faversham. The second salvo hit another plane which crashed at Leysdown, the pilot baling out. The action continued and the formation was broken in a very few minutes. A number took sudden avoiding action and two were seen flying seawards and losing height rapidly.

Towards the end of August it became very noticeable that most of the raiding aircraft approaching these shores took care to avoid areas where they had been so mauled by AA fire for the past three weeks. Raiders which came within AA guns' range at all took immediate avoiding action from the first shell-burst, or operated from very great heights. Examples of this respect for the guns were the attacks on Chatham Dockyard and the airfields at Eastchurch and West Mailing on the night of August 28th. The damage to these targets was negligible and the 'planes flew so high as to be well out of gun range. Though it was impossible for the bombers to get correct aim from such a height, they preferred not to test the AA fire; at 2 a.m., however, one of them did venture down to 13,000 feet above Chatham. He was last seen flying just above the sea with his port engine on fire and little chance indeed of reaching home.

On the last day of August there were further and more determined attacks, which were put to flight by AA fire. R.A.F. pilots witnessed a number of hits on the enemy raiders. They were able also to locate individual raiders with the help of bursts from the guns which, though the enemy were a little out of range on several occasions, served as pointers to our fighters to follow up and engage. The next day a single reconnaissance plane strayed into range of the guns at about 10.15 p.m., was engaged at once and exploded in the air.

INSTRUCTIONAL DOCUMENT ISSUED BY: HERMANN GÖRING AUGUST 19TH 1940

Regarding the continuation of the attacks on the enemy Air Force and aircraft industry, the following points will require more attention than hitherto, if our losses are to be kept down to the minimum, and the enemy Air Force swiftly and irrevocably destroyed.

Until further notice, the main task of *Luftflotten* 2 and 3 will be to inflict the utmost damage possible on the enemy fighter forces. With this are to be combined attacks on the ground organisation of the enemy bombers, conducted however in such a manner as to avoid all unnecessary losses. I will return later to the question of operations against the enemy aircraft industry.

The difficulties inherent in such a great task make it essential that while avoiding any rigid plan, the whole operation must be planned and carried through with the utmost care. This can only be possible if unit commanders at all levels are of the best type. I have therefore ordered that in future, unit commanders are to be appointed regardless of rank and exclusively from among the most suitable and capable officers. Where possible such officers should be appointed from their own unit.

Immediate steps are to be taken by *Luftflotten*, Korps and Gruppen to test the suitability of all subordinate unit commanders, with a view to effecting exchanges and removals where necessary. Not only unsuitable, but also highly inexperienced officers whose lack of experience may lead to unnecessary losses, must be replaced. Otherwise suitable but inexperienced officers must serve under a really seasoned commander until such time as the latter is prepared to recommend their promotion.

We must as far as possible avoid a state of affairs in which our aircrews are kept in constant readiness for operations, as this must inevitably fatigue our units. In the actual conduct of operations, commanders of fighter units must be given as free a hand as possible. Only part of the fighters are to be employed as direct escorts to our bombers. The aim must be to employ the strongest possible fighter forces on freelance operations, in which they can indirectly protect the bombers, and at the same time come to grips under favourable conditions with the enemy fighters. No rigid plan can be laid down for such operations, as their conduct must depend on the changing nature of enemy tactics, and on weather conditions.

Wherever feasible, fighters are also to attack the enemy on the ground. They must however be protected on such missions by succeeding waves of other fighters. Twin-engined fighters are to be employed where the range of single-engined aircraft is insufficient, or where they can facilitate the breaking off from combat of single-engined formations.

The protection of returning bombers and fighters over the Channel must be assured by specially designated fighter formations. The same applies to the defence of our own ground organisation. Young pilots not considered sufficiently experienced to fly over England could usefully carry out this latter task under the leadership of veteran pilots. The training of these young pilots and the importance of adequate supervision during their first operations are matters which cannot be too strongly emphasised.

As long as the enemy fighter defences retain their present strength, attacks on aircraft factories must be carried out under cover of weather conditions permitting surprise raids made by solitary aircraft. Such operations demand the most meticulous preparation, but can achieve very satisfactory results. The cloudy conditions likely to prevail over England in the next few days must be exploited for such attacks. We must succeed in seriously disrupting the material supplies of the enemy Air Force, by the destruction of the relatively small number of aircraft engine and aluminium plants.

These attacks on the enemy aircraft industry are of particular importance, and should also be carried out by night. Should it however not be possible to locate an industrial target because of poor visibility or bad weather conditions, some other worthwhile target must be attacked. It would appear desirable for the purpose of night operations to allocate to units particular areas which they will come to know better during each successive raid. Within this area a list of target priorities should be drawn up, so that each sortie will produce some valuable result and flights will not be wasted due to the failure of the aircraft to find one particular target. There can no longer be any restriction on the choice of targets. To myself I reserve only the right to order attacks on London and Liverpool.

Experience has shown the efficiency of light anti-aircraft defences on enemy naval vessels. Crews must therefore take care not to fly over them unless they are actually to be attacked.

My remarks concerning the allocation to units of certain areas for night raids apply also to daylight operations. The more thoroughly the units know their operational areas, the greater will be their success. This is of special importance for fighter units.

Good shooting! A German bomber brought down in a Midland farmyard.

Many barrage balloons have been shot down recently. Units should be advised not to attack such targets unless it is absolutely necessary for the conduct of the operation, or unless the attacking aircraft can do so in perfect safety.

Effective co-operation between bombers and fighters by means of conferences between unit commanders is essential for the success of combined operations and time must be allowed for this before an attack. Hurried orders and precipitate missions are impossible in the war against England; they can only lead to severe losses and setbacks.

To sum up: we have reached the decisive period of the air war against England. The vital task is to turn all means at our disposal to the defeat of the enemy Air Force. Our first aim is the destruction of the enemy's fighters. If they no longer take the air, we shall attack them on the ground, or force them into battle by directing bomber attacks against targets within the range of our fighters. At the same time, and on a growing scale, we must continue our activities against the ground organisation of the enemy bomber units. Surprise attacks on the enemy aircraft industry must be made by day and by night. Once the enemy Air Force has been annihilated, our attacks will be directed as ordered against other vital targets.

REICHSMARSCHALL HERMANN GORING
Karinhall, August 19, 1940

- C H A P T E R   2

THE BATTLE OF BRIT

O N 18 June, seeing the turn of events in Eu
Prime Minister Winston Churchill said to   .iouse
of Commons, that "the Battle of France is over, I
expect that the Battle of Britain is about to begin." He was right.
Germany was planning on blockading Britain so that no food and
supplies could get through, while pounding the British people into
submission by aerial attacks. If necessary, Operation *Seelöwe* (Sea
Lion) was to be launched to bring German troops onto British soil.
Two days prior to Churchill's speech to the House of Commons,
Adolf Hitler had already issued Directive No. 16, in which he
noted:

"As England, despite the hopelessness of her military situation,
has so far shown herself unwilling to come to any compromise, I
have therefore decided to begin preparation for, and if necessary
to carry out, an invasion of England.

"The aim of this operation is to eliminate Great Britain as a
base from which the war against Germany can be fought, and, if
necessary, the island will be completely occupied."

On 19 July, Hitler made one last attempt for a negotiated peace,
stating at the Reichstag that "... it is my duty before my own
conscience to appeal once more to reason and common sense. I
can see no reason why this war must go on... I should like to avert
the war, also, for my own people." After hearing an unfavourable
response from the British, Hitler decided to continue on with his
war plans. However, at the face of a powerful air force and navy
protecting Britain, Hitler had his doubts.

Hitler had stood triumphant in Europe. With Only the British
people, sheltered for the moment by the narrow moat of the
Channel, remained defiant. They knew, however, that the full fury
of the enemy would shortly arrive, they made ready to withstand

orst the enemy could cast upon them and, if necessary, to esist the invader with whatever weapons remained or could be quickly forged.

But while the Germans, for their part, were anxious for a speedy decision, they hoped that Britain would accept defeat without further struggle and end the war. It was not until Hitler's flamboyant peace offers had been continually ignored that the German High Command began to argue their plans for an invasion of Britain. The difficulties of the operation were realised, in particular by the Naval Staff under Admiral Raeder, who insisted that if the operation was to succeed, both the passage and the landing of troops and supplies would have to be protected from aerial attack. This demanded mastery of the air which, in turn, meant the elimination of the fighter arm of the Royal Air Force. The Germans shaped their plans accordingly and so it came about that, during the summer and autumn of 1940, Fighter Command engaged in a series of bitter air battles in defence of the British Isles. They were to prove the most fateful battles of the whole war, and the victory which followed one of the most decisive. The invasion of Britain was prevented and the base from which in turn, meant the elimination of the fighter arm of the Royal Air Force. The Germans shaped their plans accordingly and so it came about that, during the summer and autumn of 1940, Fighter Command engaged in a series of bitter air battles in defence of the British Isles. They were to prove the most fateful battles of the whole war, and the victory which followed one of the most decisive. The invasion of Britain was prevented and the base from which in time the forces of liberation were to set out and free Europe was preserved. The legend of German invincibility was destroyed and the power of the *Luftwaffe* considerably weakened.

While it was the fighter pilots of the Royal Air Force who were primarily responsible for the victory, aircrews of both Bomber and Coastal Commands made a definite influence to the upset of the enemy's plans. Unremitting reconnaissance patrols were flown over the North Sea and the Channel ports by the coastal aircraft, and as the invasion flotillas were seen assembling in the harbours and canals they were severely attacked by the bombers. Bomber Command also attacked aircraft factories in Germany and the airfields from which the enemy machines flew against Britain, while in the Western Approaches the Hudsons and Sunderlands of Coastal Command continued to protect the convoys carrying petrol and supplies to the British Isles.

Altogether in the fighter battles, the bombing raids, and the various patrols flown between 10 July and 31 October 1940 by the Royal Air Force, 1495 aircrew were killed, of whom 449 were fighter pilots, 718 aircrew from Bomber Command, and 280 from Coastal Command. Among those killed were 47 airmen from Canada, 24 from Australia, 47 New Zealanders, 17 from South Africa, 35 from Poland, 20 from Czechoslovakia and six from Belgium. But the Battle of Britain was not fought exclusively in the air. The constant devotion to duty of the ground staffs, often under the enemy's fire, was a vital contribution to the victory, while the hard work of Flying Training, Maintenance and Technical Commands greatly increased the flow of men and machines to the fighting units. A notable part was played by the men and women at the anti-aircraft gun sites, while the contribution of those who worked in the aircraft and munitions factories should also be remembered.

ADOLF HITLER'S DIRECTIVE NO.17
Directive dated August 1st 1940

From his headquarters Hitler issues Directive No. 17 for the conduct of air and sea warfare against England:

In order to establish the necessary conditions for the final conquest of England I intend to intensify air and sea warfare against the English homeland. I therefore order as follows:

1. The German Air Force is to overpower the English Air Force with all the forces at its command, in the shortest time possible. The attacks are to be directed primarily against flying units, their ground installations, and their supply organizations, but also against the aircraft industry, including that manufacturing anti-aircraft equipment.

2. After achieving temporary or local air superiority the air war is to be continued against ports, in particular against stores of food, and also against stores of provisions in the interior of the country.

    Attacks on the south coast ports will be made on the smallest possible scale, in view of our own forthcoming operations.

3. On the other hand, air attacks on enemy warships and merchant ships may be reduced except where some particularly favourable target happens to present itself, where such attacks would lend additional effectiveness to those mentioned in Paragraph 2, or where such attacks are necessary for the training of air crews for further operations.

4. The intensified air warfare will be carried out in such a way that the Air Force can at any time be called upon to give adequate support to naval operations against suitable targets. It must also be ready to take part in full force in Operation *Seelöwe*.

5. I reserve to myself the right to decide on terror attacks as measures of reprisal.

6. The intensification of the air war may begin on or after 5 August. The exact time is to be decided by the Air Force after completion of preparations and in the light of the weather.

    The Navy is authorized to begin the proposed intensified naval war at the same time.

THE LETTER THAT CHANGED HISTORY

HEADQUARTERS FIGHTER COMMAND
ROYAL AIR FORCE,
BENTLEY PRIORY,
STANMORE,
MIDDLESEX.
SECRET
May 16, 1940

Sir,

1. I have the honour to refer to the very serious calls which have recently been made upon the Home Defence Fighter Units in an attempt to stem the German invasion on the Continent.
2. I hope and believe that our Armies may yet be victorious in France and Belgium, but we have to face the possibility that they may be defeated.
3. In this case I presume that there is no one who will deny that England should fight on, even though the remainder of the Continent of Europe is dominated by the Germans.
4. For this purpose it is necessary to retain some minimum fighter strength in this country and I must request that the Air Council will inform me what they consider this minimum strength to be, in order that I may make my dispositions accordingly.
5. I would remind the Air Council that the last estimate which they made as to the force necessary to defend this country was 52 Squadrons, and my strength has now been reduced to the equivalent of 36 Squadrons.
6. Once a decision has been reached as to the limit on which the Air Council and the Cabinet are prepared to stake the existence of the country, it should be made clear to the Allied Commanders on the Continent that not a single aeroplane from Fighter Command beyond the limit will be sent across

the Channel, no matter how desperate the situation may become.

7. It will, of course, be remembered that the estimate of 52 Squadrons was based on the assumption that the attack would come from the eastwards except in so far as the defences might be outflanked in flight. We have now to face the possibility that attacks may come from Spain or even from the North coast of France. The result is that our line is very much extended at the same time as our resources are reduced.

8. I must point out that within the last few days the equivalent of 10 Squadrons have been sent to France, that the Hurricane Squadrons remaining in this country are seriously depleted, and that the more Squadrons which are sent to France the higher will be the wastage and the more insistent the demands for reinforcements.

9. I must therefore request that as a matter of paramount urgency the Air Ministry will consider and decide what level of strength is to be left to the Fighter Command for the defences of this country, and will assure me that when this level has been reached, not one fighter will be sent across the Channel however urgent and insistent the appeals for help may be.

10. I believe that, if an adequate fighter force is kept in this country, if the fleet remains in being, and if Home Forces are suitably organised to resist invasion, we should be able to carry on the war single handed for some time, if not indefinitely. But, if the Home Defence Force is drained away in desperate attempts to remedy the situation in France, defeat in France will involve the final, complete and irremediable defeat of this country.

I have the honour to be, Sir, Your obedient Servant,
Air Chief Marshal,
Air Officer Commanding-in-Chief,
Fighter Command,
Royal Air Force.

It was Air Chief Marshal Hugh Dowding who wrote the letter, putting forth his views on the sending of more fighters across the Channel for the purpose of giving France the badly needed support that they so desperately wanted. Churchill had promised the French Prime Minister Paul Reynaud who had asked for more squadrons of fighters, that they would be sent and that Britain would give support in every possible way to assist them.

The Fairy Battle and the Bristol Blenheim bombers that had originally been sent to France in the September of 1939 mainly to support the British Expeditionary Force were to prove ineffective and were totally outclassed by the German fighters. Knowing this, the Air Ministry considered sending the more effective Wellington and Whitely bombers, but the bulk of the decision makers were quite adamant that this was out of the question. The bombers were to stay in England for a strategic offensive that was "if required" to operate from their English bases.

So, the Fairy Battle single-engined light bomber's which although belonging to Bomber Command along with the Blenheim, were under the control Sir Arthur Barratt who was the R.A.F. AOC in France who had control of all aircraft. These were supported by just six squadrons of Hurricane fighters which totalled 96 and a few Gloster Gladiators. This small air force was up against the might of the advancing German *Luftwaffe* who with a commanding strength and with exceptional co-ordination constantly strafed and bombed Allied airfields and British and French troop concentrations, and like a swift, well oiled machine the Germans made a rapid advance through France.

At the beginning of the German advance, Barratt had nothing but disillusionment. Thirty-two Battles took off to curb the German advance, but thirteen of these were destroyed and eighteen suffered severe damage. 600 Squadron (Blenheim's) took off on a routine patrol of Waalhaven, and only one returned intact. On the 12th May 1940 five Battles were despatched to destroy the Bridges at Maastricht, not one of them returned, all had been destroyed. The sad story continued on May 14th, when 71 Battles took off, again on a routine bombing mission, only thirty one returned, forty had been destroyed. The next day on the 15th, Barratt tallied up the amount of aircraft destroyed, an astounding 205 light bombers and fighter aircraft had been destroyed and not even a month had passed.

The French Prime Minister Paul Reynaud made a personal appeal to Churchill. "If we are to win this battle, which might be decisive for the whole war, it is necessary to send at once at least ten more squadrons." This had put pressure on the War Cabinet in London who had already sent four additional squadrons of Hurricanes on May 12th with a further 32 aircraft the very next day. Churchill knew that one day, maybe sooner than later, the war will have reached Britain, and was insistent about supporting the British and French armies and doing all in his power in saving the Battle of France. The longer he could hold France, the more time Britain had to build her defences. Delaying the German advance was therefore of prime importance.

Dowding was informed of Churchill's intentions. He studied the forces that had already been despatched to France, he already knew that for the successful defence of Britain he would require fifty-two squadrons, this had already been depleted by the aircraft that had already been sent to France, in actual fact, he was now down to a mere thirty-six squadrons. His fears were written by way of a letter indicating the perilous position he would be placed in if this request for more fighter aircraft be sent to France. He handed the letter to his Chief Civil Servant for delivery to the War cabinet. "You know that Churchill will have to read this" to which a rather unbemused Dowding simply replied, "I know that is why I wrote it".

Hugh Dowding was summoned to the War Cabinet Room at 10 Downing Street on 15th May. Also there was Sir Archibald Sinclair who had been recently appointed as the new Air Minister, Lord Beaverbrook who had just received his appointment as Minister for Aircraft Production and Sir Cyril Newhall who was the Chief of Air Staff. "Dowding" said Churchill in his usual low toned voice, "you know that this now puts us in a very precarious position with France, I have made a commitment to the French Prime Minister that not only must we give France all the support that we can but we must support our own forces fighting in that country". Dowding remained unmoved, almost withdrawn, "I am well aware of the situation Prime Minister, but my task at hand is for the air defence of this country and it is my belief that I cannot achieve this if half my aircraft are in France".

Dowding went on to produce documents that showed the Hurricane losses since they were first despatched, and explained in considerable length that if these losses continued at this same rate, not only would he be in short supply of fighter aircraft, but of pilots as well. "We are losing aircraft at far quicker rate than we can produce them" he went on and again further emphasized the point that the thirty-six squadrons that he now had at his disposal was no where near enough for a successful defence of Britain. "We need more aircraft, and more pilots to fly them".

The following day, the 16th, Churchill flew to Paris for yet another meeting with Paul Reynaud. Again, the French Prime Minister requested help stating that unless he got it, France would fall to the Germans far sooner than he would have anticipated. He (Churchill) immediately telephoned the War Cabinet in London to request that another six squadrons of Hurricane fighters be despatched at once claiming that Dowding had informed him that only twenty-five squadrons would be required in the event that they would be needed to defend Britain. If six squadrons were sent, then that would still leave enough of a safety margin for the defence of Britain.

When the Cabinet received Churchill's request, Sir Cyril Newhall informed the Cabinet of Churchill's commitment on saving the Battle of France, and further mentioned Dowding's fears if the air strength of Britain was to be reduced. A compromising solution was reached. Six Hurricane squadrons would be sent to France, but they were to operate from bases situated on the Northern French coastal strip bordering the Channel. This way it would be possible for them to return to bases back in England each night, give added strength to the French campaign and could easily be withdrawn back to Britain should the occasion arise.

The letter above, written by ACM Sir Hugh Dowding is an interesting one. It has been reproduced it here in full hoping that you will supply your own thoughts regarding Dowding's fears.

In making a study of the above document, it is accepted that Hugh Dowding was taking the sensible approach. As he mentioned, it was the Air Council that originally decided that 52 squadrons would be the number required to successfully defend Britain, he mentions in #9 that he requests, although I would say pleads, that not a single aircraft under the 52 squadron limit that the Air Council imposed, be sent away from their bases in Britain.

Dowding would have also known that even with 52 squadrons defending Britain, there would be losses, and that judging by what was occurring in France, aircraft were being lost at a far greater rate than they were being produced. So how long could he have maintained the 52 squadrons, but, with only 32, this would have been even worse.

- C H A P T E R   3 -

HELP FROM EUROPE

THE WAR between Poland and Germany began at dawn on September 1st, 1939. Between that time and the virtual end of Polish armed resistance on Polish soil three weeks later the world looked on at the first mass bombing of a great European city. It saw what an organised air force of 3,000 'planes could do against an air force of only 300 'planes, at first organised, and then disorganised by loss and retreat. It saw the first of a series of triumphs of numbers over national faith.

Mere numbers are destructible; faith is not. When war began, the Polish Air Force had only 300 'planes of action strength. Of these, half were P-llc Fighters, a type quite slow according to modern standards. Of the rest, 36 were medium bombers of the Los P.37 type, and 60 were light bombers of the Karas type. The rest were army co-operation aircraft. But behind this small number of 'planes were great numbers of men. Poland was a country under conscription; the number of recruits to the Air Force each year was therefore considerable. If its reserves of aircraft were poor and soon to be used up, its reserves of men were enormous. If it was not possible to save the 'planes from destruction by the *Luftwaffe*, it became evident, as early as September 14th, that it would be possible to save the men. Before active Polish resistance in Poland had ended, therefore, the escape of thousands of men of the Polish Air Force - and also of the Polish Army and the Polish Navy-had been planned. This escape, both because of its size and because of its triumphs over hardship and distances, was one of the most remarkable in history.

On a day in the autumn of 1939 a young Polish airman stood by a wall in a Polish farmyard, waiting to be shot. The Nazi firing squad stood ready with their rifles, awaiting the order to fire. As the Pole stood facing them one of the rifles accidentally went off. The noise startled the rest of the Nazi firing squad, who immediately turned their heads. In that moment the Pole clambered over the wall and was gone.

The first of these men of the Polish Air Force began to reach England in early December 1939; only three months after the collapse of their country In a sense they were fortunate. Europe had not crumbled; France was still a free country; the avenues of escape were still open. For these reasons they were to be followed by many thousands of their countrymen. Meanwhile many Polish airmen had reached France. They had skied across the Carpathians. They had been through the prisons of Hungary. They had stolen boats and had rowed down the Drava River into Yugoslavia. They had come to steamer to Marseilles, they found themselves in France on a verge of defeat and disunity. So in June 1940 their escape began again. There was now only one country left for them - England. "Thousands of us" says one of them, "came away from St. Jean de Luz. Some were in uniform of the Palestine police.

The colour and spirit of France were carried to Britain by French patriots. Men of the French Fleet Air Arm work as ground staff on the airfield from which a French fighter squadron operates.

Some said they were French soldiers, some businessmen, some from turkey. And so on. Really we were all just poles wanting to fight the Germans." And so, disordered, scattered, deprived of that self-determination which had been Hitler's righteous and indignant cry in 1939, but not disunited and by no means defeated, the Poles began to come to England.

They were not alone. Nor were they the first disinherited people of the war, though their soil was the first on which war had been fought. For the Czechoslovaks the war began, not with the invasion of Poland in 1939, but with the Munich Agreement in 1938. From that moment every clear-sighted Czechoslovak saw the inevitable course of events. Immediately after Munich Czechoslovak nationals, and particularly airmen began to escape secretly from their country under cover of darkness, singly or in groups by all kinds of routes and means. They, too like the Poles, had one object. They wanted to fight Germany. The word named is worth noting. It is the key word to these pages: it is the consistent emotion binding together, in one purpose, these undefeated representatives of defeated peoples. We want to fight Germany. There is no other desire or aim.

Many Czechoslovaks, anticipating events correctly, escaped in 1938 and 1939 to Poland. Some remained there; some wandered on, through Eastern and Central Europe, on what was to be the long journey to England. When war began.

Many Czechoslovak airmen fought side by side with the Polish Air Force. When Poland fell, their way of escape was very difficult. Nevertheless, many of them reached France There they joined the only Unit open to them - the French Foreign Legion - and it was not until France's entry into the war that they were embodied in the French Air Force. During that winter, there was little air fighting, and it was only in the spring of 1940, a few weeks before the collapse of France, that the Czechoslovak National Committee and the French Government came to an agreement whereby Czechoslovak airmen obtained their independence and were to be formed into national groups. Like many other things in those days, it was almost too late. There was little time to organise. Over 100 Czechoslovak pilots were attached to various French squadrons, including the 5th Squadron of No 1 Wing of the "Cigogne" Squadron, one of the most famous French lighter squadrons of the war. In these squadrons the Czechoslovaks fought themselves to a point of exhaustion in the Battle of France. They fought with an extreme fanatical zeal and to the limits of physical endurance. There were many stories of pilots losing consciousness in the air and recovering just in time to make a safe landing Some idea of the success with which they fought may be got from Chasseurs de Ciei, a book published by Captain Accart in the autumn of 1941. On the list of fighter pilots in France, Captain Accart places a Czechoslovak pilot. Captain V., as third with 15 enemy aircraft destroyed, another Czechoslovak, Lieutenant P., as fourth and a Lieutenant V. as 12th on the list.

On the collapse of France the Czechoslovaks found themselves in a desperate position. They were scattered over a country disrupted and disorganised by defeat. The Europe at which they looked now was a very different Europe from the excited but still unified continent of 1939. Poland, Norway, Denmark, Belgium, Holland, their own Czechoslovakia and now France had gone. For them, as for the Poles, there was now only one way of escape: to England. On the orders of their Commander-in-Chief, the Czechoslovaks assembled in the South of France and even in North Africa, to begin all over again the journey to a strange country in order to continue the struggle for their fatherland.

A first group of 19 pilots arrived in England by transport aircraft on the day after the French Armistice was signed. More followed immediately. On June 21st, Dutch and Polish met chant vessels, loaded with Czechoslovak airmen, arrived in English ports, and other vessels continued to arrive until the last transport reached Liverpool on July 9th. Only three days later, on July 12th, the

Independent Czechoslovak Air Force was re-born. There was announced, with great national pride, the formation of the first Czechoslovak fighter squadron - No. 310. It practically coincided with the announcement of the first Polish Squadron, No. 300, to be formed in Britain. Like the Poles, the Czechoslovaks were

Yugoslav airmen, after the fall of their country, flew their Dornier seaplanes to Egypt and operated with the R A.F. in anti-submarine patrols over the Mediterranean. They are now being trained on British aircraft.

only just in time. They were in time for one of the great battles of history. It was a battle to decide, as we in Britain knew too well, not only whether Great Britain should survive as a free nation, but whether ultimately all Europe should survive, and it was right and opportune that the Czechoslovaks and Poles should take part in it.

But while the Czechoslovaks and Poles had been escaping through the long, tedious avenues of South Europe, Asia and Africa, much more had been happening in the north. The Norwegians, who had been flying an interesting mixture of aircraft in their short battle against Germany - using Gloster Gladiators, Curtiss Mohawks and Heinkel 115s - had also begun to arrive in England.

The story of the Battle of Norway is the story, with geographical differences, of Belgium, Holland and France. Both the Royal Norwegian Army Air Force and the Royal Norwegian Naval Air Force were very modest in size. Their aircraft were mostly obsolete types, built as early as 1925. They had few airfields, and these mostly in the coastal areas. In the summer and autumn of 1939 and the early spring of 1940, it was decided to alter this dangerous state of affairs. Both Forces were to be equipped with new types of aircraft: American Curtiss P. 36 Fighters and Douglas 8A5 Attack bombers for the Army Air Force, American Northrop N-3 P B. and German Heinkel 115 seaplanes for the Naval Air Force. Plans were also ready and funds allocated for the construction of new airfields. These plans were excellent. Their only fault was that they were too late.

When, by noon of April 9th, 1940, the Germans had succeeded in occupying all existing airfields and seaplane bases south of Narvik, it was obvious that the situation in Norway was very desperate. Against the modern forces of the *Luftwaffe*, estimated within the first weeks of the campaign to be something like 2,000 aircraft, the Norwegians had little to offer except Gloster Gladiators, which put up a gallant and hopeless fight in the defence of Oslo on the morning of April 9th, and such types as Heinkel 115 and MF11 seaplanes and Fokkers and Tiger Moths operating respectively with the Naval and Army Forces. In spite of this the Norwegian Air Forces retained their ability to operate right up to the moment when the last Allied Forces, two months after the invasion, were forced to leave Norway.

Night and day, for example, the Norwegian seaplanes, operating from fjords and ice-covered lakes, bombed and harassed German transport and troop positions on the west coast. In cooperation with Army 'planes they made communication flights, linking up isolated units of Norwegian fighting forces in fjords and valleys. They operated until the situation in Southern Norway became impossible. Then the few naval 'planes capable of the long flight were flown to the north of Norway and there continued the work of reconnaissance, bombing and ground-strafing until finally, on June 17th, 1940, the whole situation in Northern Europe was revolutionised by the collapse of France. And so the Norwegians, as the Poles and Czechoslovaks had done, came to England. The number of Poles was very large; the number of Norwegians quite small. The Poles had many means of escape, difficult and dangerous though they were; the Norwegians had very few. To navigate the North Sea to Great Britain was practically their only hope. A few were able to fly floatplanes to Scotland, but many others made the journey by sea, in small merchant vessels or in fishing smacks. Some even rowed their way across the 300 miles of water. Even then, many difficulties were still in front of them. They were too few, too disorganised and too lacking in equipment to fight immediately, so' they collected together in Canada the scattered remnants of their Air Force, and with recruits from North America formed their training headquarters known as "Little Norway." And though too late for the Battle of Britain, they later fought with the same tenacity and courage: as had brought them hundreds of miles across that dangerous water.

As time went on they became a powerful force second in numbers only to the Poles among tin Allies in Britain. In May 1941 they formed their own Naval Squadron of Northrop Floatplanes in

Iceland, from which they flew many dangerous and tedious hours of convoy escort. In July 1941, and January 1942, they formed two new squadrons of fighters, Nos. 331 and 332, fought with them in the powerful sweeps over France, and in the bloody protection combats over Dieppe, with great distinction, and later made them among the highest-scoring squadrons in Fighter Command.

One of these combats is described in a Norwegian sergeant pilot's report during the Dieppe operations: "When the Wing Commander ordered my section to attack, I dived down with my No. 1. Heading for the Dorniei to the left of a formation of four, I closed in to 400 yards and gave him a two-second burst with cannons and machine-guns as it dived to port. The bomber dived through clouds, and I followed it down. Just below cloud the enemy aircraft pulled up and set course back towards the coast just south of Dieppe. As I approached, the top rear gunner opened up with his machine-guns. His shooting was very accurate, and I was hit in wings by several bullets. Having closed to 300 yards, I opened fire. Altogether I made three attacks on the bomber - two from port beam and one from starboard beam, closing to 150 yards. As a result of these attacks the crew started baling out. I saw three men jump and all three parachutes opened. The aircraft went down in a dive and finally crashed on the beach between rocks and the water line. It burst into flames, and I saw a man, probably the pilot, standing knee height in the water beside it. Having exhausted my ammunition, I returned to base flying alone as there were no other Spitfires in the area."

No sooner had the sergeant given his report than he went straight over to his Flight Commander. "Am I flying on the next trip, Sir?" His face was one big smile when he received the answer. Soon after reaching the patrol area, numerous enemy aircraft were seen to approach flying in pairs and "fours" - a formation of six was also seen to be operating. Sgt. X. was flying as Red 2 when his section was attacked by three enemy aircraft coming out of the clouds. A number of dogfights developed and Red section became split up. Sgt. X. was flying alone when he saw two F.W. 190s coming in from astern to attack another lone Spitfire below and to port of himself. Sgt. X. dived down on the right-hand enemy aircraft, opening up with cannons and machine-guns. The range was rather long, and he saw no results from his firing, but he achieved his aim in that the enemy aircraft broke off their attack

Czechoslovak fighter pilot. On July 12th, 1940, the Independent Czechoslovak Air Force was re-born on English soil. Its first lighter squadron was destined to play a notable part in the Battle of Britain.

on the Spitfire. As he was about to pull up from his dive, he found himself attacked by five F.W. 190s coming in from port quarter and above. He tried to turn his aircraft around so as to meet the enemy aircraft head on, but had only made a half turn when a hail of bullets hit his aircraft. The F.W. 190s dived by and disappeared in the direction of the French coast. He was not hit himself, but his aircraft started burning and the engine cut out at 5,000 feet, leaving the pilot no other choice than to bale out. He released his hood and Sutton harness and then turned his aircraft upside down. By so doing he was thrown out of the aircraft, which spun down and soon after crashed into the sea. He pulled the rip-cord as soon as he was thrown clear. The parachute opened satisfactorily, and descending slowly he finally landed unhurt in the sea, having released his parachute harness on touching the water. He inflated his dinghy and entered it. Thinking that to be shot down was not such a frightful experience after all. He did not gel much time to use his experience as a sailor, as he was picked up by a motor gunboat of the Royal Navy some 15 minutes after entering his dinghy.

The Norwegians have also many pilots and navigators in Bomber Command and in British fighter squadrons as well as in Transport Command, which flies countless new aircraft from the factories of Canada and the United States across the Atlantic to the European battle-ground.

By the early summer of 1940, Holland, and Belgium too had fallen. Both had fought against the greatest odds. The story of their defeat was the story that had repeated itself, tragically, all across Europe. Faith and courage were in greater supply than weapons, and could not prevail without them. So again, in small boats in fishing smacks and even in rowing boats, Dutch and Belgian airmen made the escape to England.

A young Belgian was captured by Germans in the lighting near Saint Germain-en-Laye in the summer of 1940. He was imprisoned and escaped: he was found and re-enlisted as a munitions worker;

he performed acts of sabotage until things became too dangerous, and then escaped again. He reached the Pyrenees, walked across the mountains, and was arrested a few miles from Barcelona. From a concentration camp he made another escape, got back to Marseilles, found it too dangerous, and decided to go back to Belgium. He was then arrested by French police, and had to escape again. As he was crossing the line into Occupied France he was picked up by a French patrol, and again imprisoned. He again escaped, went to Antwerp, and, after weeks of hiding, set off for Spain. He was once more arrested, handed over to the French police, and once more got back to Belgium. His last escape was to England. With friends he set out to row across the North Sea in a small boat. On the way they were machine-gunned by German airmen; all his friends except one were killed outright or were wounded and died in the boat. The boat itself was holed by bullets, the food soaked by blood and seawater. The situation was so desperate that the two men, after unsuccessfully trying to catch sea gulls in order to drink their blood, ate toothpaste and drank sea-water. But finally, in spite of everything, they reached England.

Two Dutch pilots arrived respectively in a Fokker seaplane and a Fokker fighter, both aircraft carrying German markings, a dangerous enterprise which happily ended well. But the Dutch and Belgians, like the Norwegians, were few in numbers. They were not always to be few, and their resolution, if not so demonstrative as that of the Poles, or so buoyant as that of the Czechs, was great and clear and invincible. Happily, too, the Belgians had before the war been trained very largely on Hurricanes. The Dutch were well trained on coastal craft, of which they had succeeded in bringing a few Fokker T.8.W.S to England. The Dutch and Belgians were thus in time, and ready, for the Battle of Britain. As fighters the Belgians became very successful, and nine months there its formation one Belgian squadron had already shot down or damaged 30 enemy 'planes.

Finally, on June 26th the first Fighting French pilots arrived in England. Their position was, perhaps, the most tragic of all. France had suffered a catastrophe from which it seemed quite possible she would not recover for the rest of the century. The Poles, the Czechoslovaks, the Norwegians, the Dutch and the Belgians had reached England together with their Governments, their national unity unbroken, supported in some cases by rich resources capable of equipping them with new aircraft. They were one with each other; they had complete autonomy. The French enjoyed no such privileges. France had asked for an armistice and had found itself the victim of the most subtle of all political divisions - the Occupied and the Unoccupied. Every Frenchman who escaped to England to continue the fight was therefore in the eyes of the Vichy Government a traitor. He was liable in his absence to be condemned, as in fact many were, to death.

Dutch mechanics overhaul one of the Fokker seaplane, which, manned by Dutch naval air personnel, shared in the vital, unspectacular, and often dangerous work of Coastal Command.

In spite of all this, many Frenchmen refused to accept defeat. They came to England. They came, like the Poles and Czechoslovaks, by way of Spain and Africa and the Mediterranean; like the Norwegians and Dutch and Belgians, in merchant vessels, fishing smacks and even rowing boats across the sea.

They escaped to freedom by even stranger ways. On a day in 1940 many distinguished French officers, loyal to Vichy, were lined up on an airfield in North Africa; an airfield now in American hands. There was to be a presentation of decorations to French pilots who had distinguished themselves in the war. Among them was a French bomber pilot who had been captured by the Nazis in the French retreat, who had escaped, been hidden for weeks in a French port and had finally bicycled down through France, swimming rivers at night, until he reached Toulon. He, too, was apparently loyal to Vichy. Before the presentation of decorations there was to be a display of flying. At the assigned moment the pilot took off with the rest, circled the airfield and then quietly broke formation and flew off - to Gibraltar.

The Frenchmen who joined us came in full knowledge of what the consequences might be, not only for them, but for friends and families left behind. They came, like the rest, because they wanted to go on fighting.

- C H A P T E R   4 -
IN DEFENCE OF BRITAIN

IN THESE three stories of escape - three out of many thousands - it is possible to see the whole spirit of the unconquered peoples of Europe; the courage, the audacity, the sublime determination to be free, a pugnacious refusal to be dominated. Of these thousands of escape stories, wonderful and tragic, bitter and glorious, inspiring and humbling, the larger part can still not be told. Many of them are the greater epics of the war. All it is possible to say of such escapes, and of such a spirit of audacity, devotion and courage, is that thousands of Polish, Czechoslovak, Dutch, Norwegian. Belgian and French airmen reached Britain in the summer of 1940, and stood ready, as Great Britain also stood ready, for the new battle to begin.

But devotion, audacity and courage are not everything. Almost every schoolboy wants to fly a Spitfire; but desire without training remains a negative thing. So with the Allied airmen who arrived in this country. Their courage could never be questioned. But few of them could speak English; fewer still were trained to fly British aircraft Nor are pilots of much use without ground staff, technicians, riggers and fitters - in which most of the escaped Allies faced a serious deficiency. Thus, when the Battle of Britain was about to begin, there were relatively few Allied squadrons ready to take part in it. Behind these few squadrons, in Scotland, in Wales, in Canada, units of the escaped airmen of Europe were learning English and were re-learning, according to R.A.F. methods, how to fight and fly.

Nevertheless, some were ready. The Poles and Czechoslovaks, having begun to arrive first, were by far the largest force. By July 1940, the first two Polish bomber squadrons. Nos. 300 and 301, had been formed, though they were not to begin operating until September; and the first Polish lighter squadrons, Nos. 302 and within three weeks of each other, on August 7th and August 26th respectively, the Poles and Czechoslovaks had their first success in battle. On the first date the Polish squadrons No. 302 and 303 shot down five enemy 'planes without loss to themselves. On the second date the Czech squadron No. 310, operating in four sections of three aircraft each, met the enemy for the first time and, in a dramatic encounter, shot down two 'planes. In this encounter the Czechoslovaks were led by an English flight-commander - a combination of nationalities that has been one of the happiest features of the war.

But on September 7th, exactly a month after their first victory, the Poles did even better. That day. Indeed, they did magnificently. At about half-past four in the afternoon a formation of 16 Hurricanes of No. 303 squadron took off to meet a large enemy bomber formation protected heavily by enemy fighters. An extremely fierce encounter took place over Essex, where the Poles had kept a rendezvous with one of the most famous of all R.A.F. squadrons, the thirty-year-old No. 1. In a short time the Poles alone scored the following successes: -

10 Dornier 215s destroyed. 3 Messerschmitt 109s destroyed. 2 Dornier 215s probably destroyed. 2 Messerschmitt 109s probably destroyed. 2 Dornier 215s damaged.

For this magnificent achievement the Poles paid with three Hurricanes, from which two pilots jumped safely; the third was wounded. The day was historic. The Poles had given to the world their first real demonstration of that fanatical courage, determination and skill for which they have since become famous.

A Pole gave this description of one operation: "At 6.40 we were already up in the air. We were directed by R T to the south coast of England, and warned of a strong enemy formation making for one of the towns on the coast. We were heading for this direction and were going all out. Suddenly I noticed a lot of aircraft slightly above us. I immediately warned the Squadron Commander.

"We changed course, went into the sun and then into the attack.

It turned out that they were all Me.109s, without any bombers. Dogfights ensued immediately; we came up against odds of I to 6 and I to 7, but no one thought of that. I got hold of one Me. and started to twist and turn with him.

I then noticed that another Jerry was coming in on my tail. I made a violent turn and fell into a spin. I pulled out and then I saw an Me. about 200 yards in front. I got on his tail and opened fire without using any deflection at all. Eight machine-guns did their work. Bits flew from the Jerry, and soon he went down to the ground in smoke. I followed him down and saw how he exploded about six miles north of Dover. Soon after I saw several others falling down to earth. My squadron was at work! However, it did not last long. Jerry made back for home, and a few minutes later we too received instructions to return. We came back singly, but we all got back.

"Sometime about 12.30 we were called up a second time. This time we saw a large bomber formation approaching with an escort of fighters. We met Jerry just over the coast, but on seeing us he made a sharp turn and dived down to attack some town beneath us. The CO. led us in to head him off, and we almost succeeded. I got on the tail of a Ju.88 and pumped in round after round. Both his engines started to burn; he came down lower, turned out over the sea, and just as he crossed the coast, exploded. I circled over the burning remains, and just then I caught sight of a Defiant in a tight with an Me.109. Quite unseen by the Me., I came in under his belly and pumped in the rest of the ammunition, but it was just a bit too late, as the Defiant was already on fire and was dropping down to the water like a stone. A moment later my Me. burst into a black smoke and crashed close by his victim. A few minutes later and there was no trace on the water of either machine.

"I took a course for base and after 15 minutes landed, tired and perspiring, but happy that I had started to repay my debt to the Boche for September 1939. My CO. and the whole squadron were overjoyed. Good lads - they shook my hands and congratulated me.

"We were not given long for a rest. At 2.30 we were in the air again. Our squadron was in the second line of defence. We met Jerry well over land, but we were lower down. The CO. made a turn and we started to climb, parallel to the column of Jerries. They, meantime, were throwing out their bombs on the towns lying on the road to London. Some 25 miles outside London we were above Jerry, and we went in to attack. Just as our first aircraft opened fire, about 30 Me.109s attacked us. The last two Sections got to grips with the fighters, while the rest took on the bombers.

Defenders of Britain. From the moment of their arrival in this country, Allied airmen prepared to take part in its defence Pilots of the first Free French fighter squadron race to their aircraft squadron. No. 310.

"I was attacked by three Me.109s. I took evading action, closed down the throttle, and when the first Jerry shot past me, gave him all I could. Instantaneously he broke into flames, lost both his wings, and like a rocket went down to ground, but the other Me.s had already opened fire on me. I did a half roll, pulled back the stick, and at once lost sight of Jerry, but this manoeuvre lost me some 4-5,000 feet. I started to climb on full throttle so as to reach the nearest group of bombers, which were flying calmly along without any protection, and so far had not been attacked at all. After two or three minutes I was in a good position. At a convenient moment I opened fire and directed it on the nearest Ju.88. The rest of the Jerries fired at me with tracer bullets. This made a fine sight, as the smoke remained in the air and formed a fan-shaped pattern. My ammunition gave out after a few seconds, so I did a left climbing turn and dived down, as two machines had appeared quite near me. After losing several thousand feet I looked at my Ju.88. There he was, in flames, spinning down to the ground."

The Czechoslovaks, too, had been doing great work. In the first month of its operations, No. 310 Squadron had shot down 28 enemy 'planes, and had damaged many others. But by this time No. 310 Squadron was not alone. A second Czechoslovak squadron, No. 312, had been formed on August 29th, and many Czechoslovak pilots had been drafted to squadrons of the R.A.F. The two Czechoslovak squadrons were not only manned by Czechoslovak pilots, but were maintained by Czechoslovak ground personnel. To many of these men, excellent engineers though the Czechoslovaks are, the British aircraft were unfamiliar. They were not only maintained in first-rate condition, but the numbers of them increased, and the Czechoslovaks flew them with characteristic distinction.

And so, all through the Battle of Britain, the symbols of these two peoples were carried into combat on the fuselage of British aircraft. The scarlet and white chess-board painted on the 'planes of Polish squadrons, and the red, white and blue circles, with the white lion on a red background, which form the emblem of the Czechoslovaks. These circles are the national colours of the Czechoslovaks. The lion is the emblem of the Czechoslovak State.

The red and white chessboard of the Polish Air Force, its official emblem according to international aeronautical law, has its origin in the last war. When the Poles took possession of aircraft left behind by retreating Germans in 1918, they replaced the German iron crosses painted on the aircraft by coats of arms belonging to such districts of Poland as Warsaw, Lwow, Poznan, Kracow, and so on. Holland's record in the Battle of Britain may not have been spectacular. The public which saw day after day the great air-battles of south and south-eastern England were perhaps too enthralled and excited to remember that Great Britain was surrounded by sea, and that one of the most vital, most arduous and least spectacular jobs of the war was the job of coastal air patrol. It could not know that in one year Coastal Command would fly almost 150,000 hours and about 17,000,000 miles, over the seas from Iceland to Gibraltar, from Norway to the Outer Hebrides, bombing enemy shipping, depth-charging U-boats, protecting convoys on the sea-routes of supply; or that the Dutch, a nation rich in sea-faring history, whose sailors had been among the great navigators of all time, were taking a daily part in that vital, monotonous but often dangerous task.

It is one of the paradoxes of the war, indeed, that the small figure of 50 aircraft destroyed means more than the colossal figure of 17,000,000 operational miles. The perspective, here quite wrong, does an injustice to Coastal Command in general, and to the Dutch squadrons in particular. For the Dutch not only patrolled the seas, bombed shipping, and depth-charged U-boats. They did much work in air-sea rescue, saving by their accurate navigation and skilful plotting the lives of many fighter and bomber pilots shot down at sea. That their work was not always front-page news did not mean at all that it was not great. The work of Coastal Command pays its dividends slowly. A pilot saved from the sea may mean, perhaps, in time, long after the public has forgotten the incident, that ten more enemy aircraft have been destroyed. A convoy safely protected means more life to more people than a fallen Messerschmitt. And finally, the Dutch observer who flew back a Hudson from Norway after his pilot had been killed, may stand higher in heroism, because he had never been taught to fly, than many a pilot of a romantic Spitfire.

That observer wrote: - "One day my crew and I were detailed to do a daylight anti-shipping patrol off" the Norwegian coast. My job on this trip was navigating, and I had never flown a Hudson myself and never thought I could.

"We took off at about noon and set course towards the Norwegian coast. Most of the trip was done under bad weather conditions, cloud base was about 800 feet, and it was raining steadily. But as we reached a point 30 miles off the enemy coast, the weather cleared and the rain stopped.

We flew on a course parallel to the coast in search of enemy convoys. After about 15 minutes' flying, we sighted one - two medium-sized supply ships and two escort vessels or flakships. We dived into the clouds and kept nipping in and out to make out the lie of the land. We finally decided to attack the biggest supply ship from the rear. We got into position, shut our throttles, and glided out of the clouds to make our bombing run. At first they didn't seem to realise what was happening, but as we got within 300 yards' distance, they opened up with light and heavy machine-guns and cannons. The fire was heavy and became more and more accurate. We swooped over the ship, released our bombs and then tried to make our getaway. Then things began to happen.

"There was a hell of a bang - one of their cannon shells had hit us right by the cockpit; just afterwards another hit us a little behind, almost severing the control wires, as we learnt later. At the same moment the pilot - a chap weighing 13 stone - collapsed. The shell had exploded by his left leg; after a few seconds he was unconscious, and within a few minutes bled to death. I was

A Belgian pilot flew back to his country, at immense risk, to rescue the flag of the Belgian Air Force. The flag is being presented here to the first Belgian squadron to be formed on British soil.

standing close to him and reached over his body to seize the controls.

"There was a hell of a bang - one of their cannon shells had hit us right by the cockpit; just afterwards another hit us a little behind, almost severing the control wires, as we learnt later. At the same moment the pilot - a chap weighing 13 stone - collapsed. The shell had exploded by his left leg; after a few seconds he was unconscious, and within a few minutes bled to death. I was standing close to him and reached over his body to seize the controls.

"I pulled hard on the stick to get the aircraft out of the dive- that was difficult enough- and then tried to engage the automatic pilot, but the damned thing wouldn't work. Well, that looked nice, leaning over a dead pilot, precariously holding the Hudson in the air, having to go back over 300 miles and land the aircraft! It seemed quite impossible. The rest of the crew came to my help, dragged the dead pilot out of his seat and helped me get into his place. And then for home. It wasn't easy, but finally we made it, and we saw an airfield near the coast we were very glad.

"But now the worst part, landing 10 tons of aircraft at a speed of 100 miles per hour. So, sweating heavily, we tried to make our first landing run, undershot and tried once again. Twice it was unsuccessful - the Flying Control people must have had kittens by then - and then the third time we were lucky, and managed to make a fairly decent landing. I felt like kneeling down and kissing mother earth. Can you imagine how I enjoyed the first pint of beer?"

In this way, solidly, conscientiously, with heroic determination, the Dutch took their part.

Two other countries in Europe had now joined the dispossessed. Greece, which had waged against Italy a campaign of such heroic success that the thrill of it touched the world, and Yugoslavia, peopled by hardy romantic peasants in a territory of black mountains where a magnificently organised war against

Germany and Italy still goes on, had at last been occupied by a Germany still seeking strategic Lebensraum. To the Grecian war it had unfortunately not been possible to send more than a few squadrons of British aircraft, so that the Greek story became, like the Yugoslavian story with it and the stories of Czechoslovakia, Belgium, France, Holland, Norway and Poland before it, the old story of faith without arms.

Greece and Yugoslavia were terrorised, as countries north of them had been terrorised, by an exhibition of robot armed force. Belgrade was treated to the savagery that had struck Warsaw and Rotterdam, London and Coventry. The way of the Greeks and the Yugoslavs was as clear as the light of morning: to go on resisting, in secrecy or in exile, long after it had seemed impossible. So, inspired by these ideals, two more small countries, passionate in national idealism, joined the Poles, the Czechoslovaks, the Dutch, the Norwegians, the Belgians and the French in the fight for the right to be left alone, in freedom, to live their national lives. For the Yugoslavs, chances of escape were certainly not great; but from their seaplane base at the beautiful little town of Kotor, in the great fjord-like harbour on the Dalmatian coast, a few crews managed to get away. From there they reached Egypt, where they were able to carry on the fight alongside the R.A.F., using their Dornier 22 seaplanes to help in submarine patrols over the Mediterranean. Even to day a few Yugoslav patriots are still escaping to join their countrymen and help expand the Yugoslav Air Force These men are training on British aircraft and will be formed before long into operational units.

The Greeks who escaped to British territory proceeded to do in the Middle East what six exiled nations had already done in Great Britain They re-formed, re-equipped, re-trained themselves; they began to learn English - which, thanks to a Scots teacher, many of them spoke with a strong Scottish accent; they were becoming a new striking force, part of an infinitely stronger organisation than the little Greek Air Force that had vainly resisted the *Luftwaffe* with such notable courage. Greeks who had been evacuated from Greece and Greeks who had made their own escapes, Greeks from Egypt and all over the Middle East, now joined themselves together with the ardent spirit that had for so long defied the Italians. Among them was a young Greek soldier who had been wounded three times in the Albanian campaign, whose brother had been killed, and whose ship had been sunk by bombs soon after leaving its Greek port. As soon as he reached Egypt he demanded transfer to the new Greek Air Force. His spirit was typical.

As these new Greek units became trained, new Greek squadrons were formed. A Greek squadron of Hurricanes soon began to protect Mediterranean shipping and to raid convoys. A second squadron, equipped with Blenheims, made submarine patrols, long-range reconnaissance. Many of these Greeks, now flying British aircraft, had already, flown, like many Poles and Czechoslovaks, 2,000 or 3,000 hours. They held Greek decorations. Now they began to earn British decorations. A Wing Commander dive-bombed enemy airfields in the Iraq campaign; the exploit earned him the D.F.C. While these things were happening, more and more Greeks came to join the new Greek Air Force. Soon there were enough of them to make it possible for a complete Greek depot to be formed. Greek technical officers, administration officers, medical officers, Greek N.C.O.s and ground staff - they began to prove, once again, that national ardour cannot be squeezed to death between the fingers of aggressors. They, too, had only one object - a living Greece.

So two more exiled Air Forces were joined, still fighting, with the R.A.F. And while they were escaping by sea and air to Malta, Crete and the North African mainland, things of importance were still happening in Britain.

On November 7th, 1941, the first Free French Squadron, No. 340 Fighter Squadron, was formed. It had been nearly 18 months since the first Free French pilots had reached England. The Poles had been able to form their first exiled squadrons in about nine months, the Czechoslovaks in about ten months, from the outbreak of war The Dutch, in spite of defeat in the spring of 1940, had been able to re-form and light by the summer.

The position of the French was not easy. Metropolitan France was a big country, slit in half. The French Empire was colossal, occupying, as a glance at the African map in particular will show, rich and strategically important areas of the world. A divided France, with a divided and bewildered Empire, without certainty of leadership, was a political tool of dangerous importance. The defeat of France had led to a disruption: it was the vortex of the war. Into this vortex, in the summer of 1940, Great Britain might have been dragged down.

It was therefore immensely to the credit of the de Gaullists that they should choose to fight from England, where the cause was by no means certain of success, rather than remain under domination at home. It was significant also that they gathered together in England under the emblem of the Croix de Lorraine, first adopted as the badge of the Forces Francoises Lihres in 1940. That dual cross, in no sense a national emblem or part of the national flag, expressed precisely the same spirit of liberation once expressed by Jeanne d'Arc, who, too, carried the Cross of Lorraine. It had a history, in France alone, of 700 years. Brought from the East in 1241 by Jean d'Alluye, it was kept at the Hospital for Incurables at Bauge. The first Duke of Anjou, Louis, had a great devotion for the relic, and introduced it into the Coat of Arms of the House of Anjou. At Anjou it is part of the splendid tapestries of the Apocalypse and several decorative themes in the cathedral. When Rene, Duke of Anjou, became Duke of Lorraine in 1431, after his marriage, he incorporated the double cross into the coat of arms of the new Duchy. From that time onward the cross, known formerly as the Cross of Anjou, it became the Cross of Lorraine.

So on a spring day of 1942, exactly 700 years after Jean d'Alluye had brought the cross from the East, you might have seen a burly Frenchman, pipe in mouth, in the dark blue uniform of the French

Air Force, doing his best to make a rough design of the cross in stones, on a ground of sand, outside the dispersal hut of the first Free French Squadron in England. With typical French provincial love of a piece of property, this Frenchman had neatly lined out the path with stones on either side and had painted them white. The cross, loo, was painted white. The sand was raked smooth. Plump, dark, pipe-smoking, this Frenchman might have been any French provincial artisan painting up his garden anywhere from Dieppe to Bordeaux, from Toulon to Morlaix, on a warm spring day. All about him, on the perimeter track where Spitfires were lined in readiness for sweeps over France, Frenchmen from all corners of the earth were also in process of making a little piece of England as much like France as they could.

If you put the point of an imaginary pair of giant compasses in Berlin and place the other point in Iceland you can draw, going southward, an interesting circle. It will pass the British Isles, cut through French Morocco, Algiers, Libya, Egypt, Syria, Iran, the Caspian Sea, the great Central Russian plain, Stalingrad, Moscow and Leningrad, and will ultimately emerge al Murmansk. Inside this circle lie Germany, Italy, Austria, Rumania and half a dozen subjected nations; all along the edge of it, closer and closer, more and more powerful, lie the forces of opposition. In that circle lies the strategy of the European war.

When the war began there was no circle. Confused and bloody spots of savagery broke out at disconnected points on the map of Europe: Poland, Norway, France, Belgium, Holland, finally Greece and Yugoslavia. There was a bloody spot over Britain. As the war progressed an inner circle was formed, acquired and dominated by Germany. Out of this inner circle, with its horrors of persecution, the Gestapo, the hostages, the bloody curfews, the savage reprisals, there escaped in ones and twos, in hundreds, sometimes in thousands, the men who are the subject of these pages. They escaped to help form, in time, the outer circle as it stands to day. This circle is no longer symbolic, but real. It is not

This Dutch ground crew is bombing up a Fokker T.8.W., one of the aircraft they succeeded in bringing over to England.

simply a circle of faith, but of arms. Its power consists not in hope, but in ships, in Spitfires, in Wellingtons, Halifaxes, Lancasters and Stirlings, in Mosquitoes and Bostons, in Hudsons and Flying Fortresses, in men and guns. The encirclement of inner Europe is no longer an indignant myth of Nazi propaganda: it is no longer the retaliatory encirclement of Great Britain. It becomes a fact of geography, men and arms.

The men of the Allied Air Force are relatively in numbers, a small part of that completed circle, now powerfully reinforced by the United States. Their greatness and their achievement are not, however, in the accomplished thing, but in their port in its accomplishment. Their greatness lies in the fact that, when the war was confused, desperate and even on the verge of being lost, they decided to make the immense personal sacrifice needed for them to remain actively lighting. Their greatness lies in the fact that they rejected personal safety and commitments for a voluntary and dangerous exile; in the fact that they left families, parents and friends under enemy occupation and persecution, knowing that they might suffer because of them, simply for the uncertain chance of being able to avenge, in the air, the defeat of their native countries.

The exploits of flying men and of aircraft tend, as time goes on, to repeat themselves. The exploits of Spitfires run to a pattern; the long journeys of Catalinas over the Atlantic become as alike as the voyages of ocean liners. It becomes harder and harder to extract, from thousands of combat reports, a new exploit more illuminating and heroic than one which has already happened. It becomes easier to take the great event of yesterday for granted. For this reason the exploits of the men of the Allied squadrons may seem to be of the same pattern as those of other men. But theirs, in fact, was always a different achievement. It demanded always an extra personal sacrifice; it asked more of the imagination; it was full of potential distress, not only for the man himself, but for those he loved most at home. It demanded an endurance that could not be alleviated by family meetings, the family fireside and all the comforts of home. It demanded all, and always, the patience of the exile.

What of the future? The result of this great sacrifice cannot be temporary. The infiltration into the insular life of Great Britain by thousands of young Poles, Czechoslovaks, Norwegians, Dutch, Belgians and Frenchmen must do something to affect that life. In peace we talk of war; in the middle of war we begin to talk of peace. The plans for peace are often grandiose, vague and illusory. But in the presence of thousands of young foreign airmen in Great Britain we have a fact from which a new international understanding, idealistic yet free from antipathetic ideologies, might grow to benefit the world. These men have lived in Britain and, while fighting for their own countries, have fought for Britain and the ideals which will live while Britain lives.

We on our side must never forget this. But these men could never have fought here without British aircraft, flown from British airfields, built by British hands and brains and made by British coal and steel. They, too, on their side, will never forget.

Living in Britain, these men have seen our life familiar with British customs. They have married British girls. Already some of them have families. The roots of Scandinavia and Central Europe reach out and take new life in the English midlands, in Edinburgh and London in the mountains of Scotland and Wales, in the blitzed cities. From America come more men, to find in English valleys the very place-names, sometimes the very idioms, of their own country. These men are taken into British homes, given British hospitality. Men from Texas and Colorado, born to immense distances, fly over a little country where the landmarks are like a tangle of loose stitches. Men from the Middle West help to gather in the harvest of English corn.

If there is to be a better international understanding in the future, its roots are here. They are the roots of the living men. Wars are won on the battlefield, on the sea and in the air: they are lost at the conference table. In this war, more than any war in history, nations have endured a common experience. The bomb falls on the home, from Oslo to London, Warsaw to Plymouth, Belgrade to Liverpool, Rotterdam to Coventry, Stalingrad to Canterbury. The Cathedral, the house, the flat, the café, the hospital, the school- none of them in inviolate any longer. They have never been so few non-belligerents, so few neutrals as now. We all make the common sacrifice.

The story of the Allied Squadrons, small perhaps against the complete epic of the twentieth-century revolution, is an important part of that sacrifice.

In 1940, Mr. Winston Churchill made to France the offer of a Franco-British union by which the citizens of each country would become citizens of the other. Today, as the Allied Squadrons help to account for the 170 enemy aircraft shot down over Dieppe, as Poles become "honorary citizens" of the German cities they bomb in their Wellingtons, as the Norwegians rise from their small beginnings to second place in numerical strength, as Czechoslovaks, Belgians, Greeks, Dutch, French and Yugoslavs carry on the air war from the shores of the Mediterranean to the fjords of Norway, there is being made in the air, if we care to see it, the possibility of a new union on earth. It could be a union of men, not words; it could be the new inheritance of the disinherited.

On a night in March, 1941, the Battery Commander responsible for the AA defence of the Widnes area made out the following incident report:

"21.25 hours - An aircraft blew up in the air, bearing 290.

"21.30 hours - An aircraft was seen surrounded by a shell burst and lit up with an orange glow.

"21.35 hours - An aircraft crashed in flames, bearing 240 - distance about 3 miles."

The 'plane referred to in the last two extracts, a Heinkel III, pitched in a sports field on the town's outskirts. It burned luridly, consuming the pilot; but three members of the crew who baled out were captured. The 'plane had first been hit by an anti-aircraft shell, causing loss of height and speed; then a night-fighter had picked it up and fired from point-blank range; and finally, when its fall had become a scream of punctured engines, the 'plane had struck a barrage balloon cable.

Greece lives in the spirit and deeds of such pilots as this - men who after blatantly defending their country against the Luftwaffe escaped to form Greek squadrons of the R.A.F. and take part in the victorious middle east campaigns.

That is an example of the Air Defence of Great Britain - A.D.G.B. - in the full flower of co-operative function. Fighter Command is the main defence of Britain; but Fighter Command could not survive without AA Command, and that is what we are concerned with here - the story of our anti-aircraft guns and searchlights.

It isn't easy to shoot down a 'plane with an anti-aircraft gun. With a field gun, sitting still, shooting at a fixed target, mathematically you only expect one hit in a hundred rounds. There are several reasons why this should be so; for instance, atmospheric conditions, such as a belt of moisture, deflect the shell in its flight; and with each shot the charge burns a little differently.

The anti-aircraft problem is more complicated. Instead of sitting still, the target is moving at anything up to 300 mph with the ability to alter course left or right, up or down. If the target is flying high it may take 20 or 30 seconds for the shell to reach it, and the gun must be laid a corresponding distance ahead. Moreover the range must be determined so that the fuse can be set, and above all, this must be done continuously so that the gun is always laid in the right direction. When you are ready to fire, the 'plane, though its engines sound immediately overhead, is actually two miles away. And to hit it with a shell at that great height the gunners may have to aim at a point two miles farther still. Then, if the raider does not alter course or height, as it naturally does when under fire, the climbing shell and the bomber will meet. In other words the raider, which is heard apparently overhead at the Crystal Palace, is in fact at that moment over Dulwich; and the shell which is fired at the Crystal Palace must go to Parliament Square to hit it. It is like shooting a pheasant with a rifle in the dark. Perfect team work is necessary. Any single man, from the man who sees the 'plane and decides it is hostile (a testingly responsible decision), to the man who pulls the firing lever, can wreck the shoot.

So it is not bad going that three times our AA gunners have shot down more than 50 German 'planes over this country in a week, and that during one week they shot down 70. During their most successful 24 hours, August 15th, 1940, they destroyed 23 enemy 'planes, this bag being contributed to by gun batteries in seven towns from Dundee to Dover. Eleven were brought down at Dover, seven on Tyneside and Teeside, and the rest at Southampton, Harwich and Dundee.

A fortnight later, on August 31st, 21 were shot down, 16 of them in 90 minutes during the evening blitz. During the whole of 1940, AA batteries in the British Isles shot down 444 enemy aircraft. The odd half represents the AA gunners' share in an enemy bomber, which was finished off by fighters after it had been winged by a near miss from a ground battery. These figures do not include the many probables, which limp out over the coast and crash unwitnessed in the sea.

During the first two years of war just on 600 'planes were shot down by AA fire over this country, and during the same two years fighter 'planes destroyed 3,900. So, roughly speaking, the guns bring down one plane for every six shot down by fighters.

The ratio varies. In March and April, 1941, it was one to the guns and two to the fighters. Every third aircraft shot down was shot down by the guns.

A more important criterion of efficiency is how our AA fire compares with the German AA fire. This is a difficult question to answer.

But certainly it is true that our bomber losses are lower than the enemy's known losses in proportion to the number of 'planes used. Let us take one example of our losses in man-power, for the loss of trained crews is in every way more serious than the loss of machines. In the big four-figure raid on Cologne, the target was attacked by about 6,000 men (slightly less than the bayonet strength of a Division of infantry). They suffered between 300 and 400 casualties only. This in spite of the fact that our bombers usually attack at lower heights than the enemy in order to ensure greater accuracy, and in consequence tend to provide better targets than the German bombers over here. In contrast, on the great day of September 15th, 1940, the Germans attacked with between 2,000 and 3,000 men, and lost between 600 and 700 of them.

German respect for our AA defences started low but has flourished and grown. The first-class enemy pilots keep on with their job, the others don't. If a man is wondering whether he has got to take avoiding action he is not going to concentrate on hitting Buckingham Palace or the War Office; he is going to be jinking about, and his aim will be disturbed at a critical moment. That is one of the main functions of Anti-Aircraft Command - to disturb the aim and deter the faint-hearted. The number of 'planes shot down is by no means the only measure of anti-aircraft efficiency and value.

Life is easy when there are plenty of 'planes to shoot down; it is not so obviously worth while to men who have had to wait months, perhaps years, for the opportunity to fire at an enemy 'plane at all. Months, or years, of the most demoralising dullness, during every hour of which it is necessary to behave as if the enemy were expected at any minute. And when, finally, the enemy 'plane does arrive, it may be only possible to fire at it for a few seconds; or, perhaps, because our own 'planes are in the neighbourhood, they may not be allowed to fire at all.

Conditions of life in the AA Command are much more difficult than is generally imagined even by the rest of the Army. The men must be in constant and instant readiness, all through the day; some of them all through the day and night; some of them all through the night with maintenance work during the day. They are in little pockets all over the country, many of them under junior N.C.O.s and miles from the nearest farmhouse. A few, even at this stage of the war, have not yet had the chance to fire their guns. It is therefore a dull life and must often seem a meaningless one, full of petty, and sometimes not so petty, hardships and discomforts. This book is an account of their work and the trials they have to face, and an appreciation of their achievement.

- CHAPTER 5 -
THE BUILDING OF THE ROOF

T HE TASK of developing AA defences is not new. It had to be done in the last war. But the job in 1914 was very different from the job in 1939. In 1914 there was no semblance of a black-out until October 1st, and on that day 12 AA guns and 12 searchlights were deployed in the London Area. These merely token defences were not so inadequate as they seemed, because air-power was in its infancy; and the attack was unlikely to be more terrible than the defence. But the Germans were already thinking of terror raids.

In September 1914, the Chief of the German Naval Staff wrote a minute saying, "I hold the view that we should leave no means untried to crush England, and that successful air raids on London, in view of the already existing nervousness of the people, would prove a valuable means to that end." On January 9th, 1915, the Kaiser gave his permission for attacks to start, these attacks to be "expressly restricted to military shipyards, arsenals, docks, and, in general, military establishments; London itself was not to be bombed."

When the raids came they caused a great loss of working time and not a little upset. The first place to be bombed - King's Lynn on January 19th, 1915 - was the subject of a report from the Zeppelin commander to the effect that he had been "heavily attacked by guns and engaged by searchlights." Such defences, however, did not exist, and his report gives some indication of his diffidence. Nevertheless, these comparatively feeble raids had a considerable effect, not only in slowing up munition production but in keeping back from France sorely needed fighter aircraft and AA guns. Gradually the defences got the upper hand; the beginning of the end of the Zeppelins came when Leefe Robinson earned his V.C. by shooting down the SL. 11 near Cuffley. Soon the Germans were routing themselves clear of the London defences.

By 1918 these consisted of 284 guns, 377 searchlights, and 11 fighter squadrons. But in 1919 A.D.G.B. was disbanded, and until 1922 there was no AA protection in this country except for one very small regular brigade and searchlight battalion - 2/3,000 men in all. In 1922, four heavy Anti-Aircraft Regiments (then called brigades) and two searchlight battalions were formed, all in and around London. Most of their recruits came from the Banks, the Insurance Companies, Lloyd's, and one or two large concerns like Vickers and the Wandsworth Gas Company. They were very much under strength and recruiting was a problem they could not solve. At the first post-war camps in 1923 there were about 30 men to represent batteries which should have had 150 men. Certainly there was little enough inducement to join except for the incorrigibly military or determinedly sociable. They had to spend a great deal of their first camp period in humping ammunition over two and a half miles of sand dunes. They not only carried their own ammunition, but that of the regulars who followed them to camp, and they had next to no transport. Practice was thus negligible.

They went to camp again the following year, much increased in strength, but still saddled with so many fatigues that they had little time for shooting. Equipment was meagre in the extreme, money was always tight, and it was not unusual for units to spend considerable sums of money in buying their own equipment.

By 1925 the political situation started to look less favourable, and very slowly a start was made to rebuild the air defences. There were now two regular anti-aircraft brigades - about 5,000 men - who spent half their year running camps for territorials. The regulars were not designed for the defence of this country but to go abroad with an expeditionary force. Things gradually began to build up; by 1936 there was one AA Division, and a second Division was formed. By 1938 there were five, and they were brought together under one AA Corps. In 1939 there were seven Divisions and the Corps became a Command.

General Sir Frederick Pile A.A Command.

This seems a lot compared with 1914; but no comparison is valid. Only eight months later the German Air Force killed 30,000 people in Rotterdam in half an hour. In September 1939, an air attack on any one of the countless targets crowded into this island was not only possible but considered highly probable. The 1939 establishment was therefore by no means excessive. Moreover, the greater part of the men were recent recruits, and the later flood of new or renovated guns was still only a trickle. This makes it the more remarkable that a year later a formidable artillery served by fully skilled gun-crews was ready to meet the assault of the *Luftwaffe*. Credit for this jump from infancy to maturity must be shared among many people, from the men and women who made the guns and shells to the General who controlled the destinies of AA Command. General Sir Frederic Pile, who took over this job a few weeks before the outbreak of war, has made the family created by his predecessor grow with an efficiency and energy for which both his command and the public have good cause to be grateful. The modern commander has an administrative job which would tax the talents of a captain of industry, on top of a military job which is always presenting new possibilities and problems. He has to consider everything from the finding of labour to build huts for the A.T.S. to the fragmentation of metals under certain conditions. To revive an echo of a conundrum of 1914-18 vintage, though bread is the staff of life, the life of the staff is no longer a long loaf. Part of the success of AA Command is due to the fact that General Pile has known how to get the best out of his staff and that he has been to scientists the kind of patron they dream about. All their ideas have been tried at least once, and tried quickly. That is why in so short a time the basis of our AA defences has been changed from a bluff to a buckler.

CHAPTER 6

STUDYING THE
ENEMIES METHODS

AS PART of the process of trying to keep one jump ahead of the enemy, officers from AA Command have often flown with our bomber crews. These officers are not in any sense passengers; they are trained as air gunners, but their main job is to observe and report on the enemy's ground defences and how they can be best avoided, and to see what lessons can be learned from the enemy.

The officers originally chosen were sent on a short course at a Searchlight Wing, where their knowledge of searchlight methods was brought up-to-date and amplified.

But the main emphasis of the course was on cultivating their powers of observation. For instance, they were set down on a hillside, each with binoculars, and told to observe and comment on events in a small barbed-wire encampment some distance away. A man came out of the camp and sat down reading a newspaper which reflected brightly and would give away the position from the air. An A.T.S. girl came up to the camp, spoke to the sentry and was admitted. Rifle fire broke out in some woods near by and the camp was captured.

The class had to write a reconstruction of these and the other events; and they had to draw a panorama of the scene showing how they would have attacked the camp, and why. All this, of_ course, was designed to build up the spirit of restless inquisitiveness which is the body and soul of reconnaissance. They were taken out at night and shown what all kinds of searchlights looked like, and then they were sent on a three-day course in which guns were fired at a point near them to train them to distinguish the different kinds of fire. They were then posted to R.A.F. operational training units for a further course in air gunnery. Here they learned to operate aircraft guns and turrets. They learned to cure gun stoppages and write reports sitting in the dark in a confined space. They had to practice in a turret in a dark room until they passed the tests. It was a condensed air gunner's course, without radio, but thorough enough to entitle them to wear the air gunner's single wing badge.

Immediately afterwards they were posted to different Bomber stations and joined their crews. The air observer sits in the front gunner's turret. To get into it he clambers over the bomb-aimer's panel, opens the bulkhead door and the two turret doors and swings himself in by a bar in the roof of the turret. There is not much room to move about. The seat is just large enough and placed between two ammunition tanks on which he can rest his elbows during the flight. There are little holes in the top of the tank through which you can see the ammunition being fed into the guns.

The guns are at eye level with a ring sight in between them. To rotate the turret and fire the guns the observer has two handles worked on rather the same principle as the handle-bars of a motorcycle. When you twist the handles the turret swings round, and to tire the guns there is a trigger appendage to the grips.

The air observers are not usually instructed to look for anything in particular, but to make a general and detailed report of everything they see. On a clear night they may be able to study the enemy's fire control methods and searchlight deployment for more than half an hour while approaching the target, and they achieve impressively detailed results when they are under fire. On the first few trips their impressions tend to be sketchy, but with each flight they become more valuable. Time is the important thing; if they know exactly what time a thing happened they can check with the navigator afterwards exactly where it was on the ground. They jot their notes by a dim orange lamp which shines over their shoulder.

Here are typical extracts from reports made by one officer who is forty years old; before the war he was an electrical engineer. These extracts are, of course, necessarily jumbled.

"The gun flashes on the ground were of two distinct and definite colours, i.e., yellow and deep orange. As far as we could see, the latter were from the very heavy guns."

"As far as we could see the guns were not being directed but were firing a barrage at all heights from 12,000-18,000 feet."

"Very small number of guns, probably not more than 10 of, say, 88-mm calibre.

There was no obvious form of fire control being used. The shells were bursting in all parts of the sky above the target, and at all heights between 14,000-16,000 feet, but none near enough to cause us any anxiety."

What are these reports used for? They go to Bomber Command and are sometimes used in briefing crews who make subsequent raids on the same area. They go to the military intelligence directorate to confirm or amplify their other sources of information about the same areas. They go to the men who plan our own AA defences; and - perhaps most interesting of all they go to the scientists, to the AA Command's Operations Research Group.

AA Command has two main research stations devoted entirely to its problems and employing some hundreds of scientists. The Operations Research Group consists of about 70 scientists and statisticians who work in a three-storied suburban vicarage and overflow into two small army huts. The air observers reports are dealt with mainly by the statisticians. If the observer reports 14 illuminations over Brest and gives an estimate of the number of searchlights visible over a certain area, the statisticians may then be able to work out the density and extent of the searchlight belt. The scientists have more than one observer's report to go on, of course. There were eight on the first Paris raid as well as all the R.A.F. reports. But naturally the AA officers, with their gunnery experience, can usually provide a better picture of ground defences than the airmen. Suppose the observers' reports suggest that the enemy are using some new kind of equipment; this intelligence might be the basis of a raid on the enemy coasts.

Perhaps an observer may report the use of red and blue searchlights. Under certain weather conditions this may be an illusion produced by ordinary white lights. But, if the same lights are reported in the same places on different nights in different weather, it is worth investigating. Perhaps we have rather exaggerated the impact of the observers' reports on the scientists' work, the value and extent of which it is difficult to over-estimate. The scientists also do their own field work. They have recording units which go and stay with the guns. The units consist of five men and a recording van. They test their theories and designs as translated into action. Since the war started the progress in research and its results have been great. The guns themselves are much the same, but the methods of fire control have advanced as far as the Rolls Royce from the hansom cab.

THE DOG FIGHTS

ERIAL DOG-FIGHTING with many machines locked in combat and whirling round in a tremendous wrestling match, is the kind of thing visualized by most people when they hear about victories of Royal Air Force fighters over enemy raiders. This is often one stage of the battle, but although it may be the decisive stage, it is not the crucial stage. The crucial stage in all modern air defence operations, especially at night, concerns the finding of the enemy. As in most things, it is not the brilliant, dramatic final spectacle that counts most, but the quiet and careful preparation for it. And this is most concerned with the search. Finding the enemy is the real crux. Find the enemy and with the modern aircraft of the 1940's, and the Royal Air Force pilots the chance are that he won't get away.

Look at the problem, there is a huge air space over these islands and over our coastal waters to be watched. If an enemy aircraft attempts to enter that air space: its presence must be detected, its nationality recognised, its course determined, and the fighter command warned. Defending an airline is not like defending a landline or a coastline.

Ships and tanks work only on one level. Aircraft work on any level within five or six miles. So there is an extra thing to be observed - an extra dimension. Air war, in fact, is three-dimensional war, and therefore air defence calls for three-dimensional search. The enemy machine is a needle in an extraordinarily large haystack.

And the look at the tremendous difficulty of spotting another aeroplane from the air. The fighter pilot is boxed in his narrow cockpit with deafening engine almost in his lap. Above the noise of that engine he hears nothing. The wings and fuselage of his machine limit his arc of view. From this extraordinarily inefficient watchtower he must try to spot the enemy.

Battle of Britain London contrails

One can hardly exaggerate the difficulties of search from the air. That is why, in the finding of the enemy, so much depends upon the people on the ground. There are the Observer Corps, the sound locators, the searchlights and the anti-aircraft guns. In the final stage of battle it is the pilots eye, which count. But all up to that stage all indication must be indirect and must come from these people on the ground.

Observer Corps, sound locators, searchlights and anti-aircraft fire; these are the information departments which tell first the operations room, and then the fighter pilot, where to go to make contact with the enemy. They note his movements and positions. They warn the headquarters and operation room and fighter command. And only in the last stage does the fighter pilot, sitting boxed up in his plane at many thousands of feet above the earth, half blinded by the machine around him, half deafened by the engine, receive his directions and know where he must go in order to bring the enemy to battle. He will then look and trust to his own eyes for picking the enemy out at close range. At that point the responsibility swings from those careful, quiet observers on the ground to the man in the air. When the pilot gets the word there is a jump in speed. Things happen in seconds instead of minutes.

Much depends on the approach, for at the moment when fighting aeroplane's are attacking they are extremely vulnerable. If a section of fighters is going in to attack a formation of enemy fighters, they must concentrate in their task of getting within range and taking accurate sight, if there is another formation of enemy fighters above, that formation will try to come down on the tails of our machines just as they are attacking, when their attention is fully occupied. And that is usually the start of a dogfight. For the moment a fighter pilot sees the enemy coming down on an attempt to be the first to gain a firing position.

Sections of fighters attack according to one of many predetermined tactical plans. But when the combat is joined it usually develops a mix-up, when each man has to fight his own battles. If you imagine a close-range combat with 100 or 150 machined engaged you can understand that detailed tactical processes are limited, although there is always a general tactical plan, of course.

Individual aircraft may be moving at anything up to 400 miles an hour, and there may be combined speeds, when machines approach one another, of 700 miles an hour- about the speed of a falling bomb.

The aeroplanes will be turning, diving, climbing all seeking urgently to get decisive results quickly. The collision risks are enormous. The difficulty of sorting out the plane of battle- or even of keeping an eye on which are friendly - is almost insuperable.

The demands made on the human machine as apart from the air machine are drastic. But we know that our own pilots do well in these dogfights. They usually gain the day, and the enemy aircraft with which they make contact do not often go home. It is worth remembering that those final successes in the earlier stages are simply the transmission of accurate information provided by the watchers on the ground.

CHAPTER 8

AN AIR BATTLE OVER THE ENGLISH CHANNEL
Article by Oliver Stewart

AT THE beginning of August Germany began massed air attacks against English Channel shipping and ports. In this contribution Oliver Stewart gives an account of one of the first raids, and expresses the opinion that if the attacking German formations become too big the enemy will find them a source of weakness and they will be cut to pieces by a 'well-drilled, highly proficient formation'.

Ever since the beginning of the war it had been evident that the Germans hoped to destroy our shipping by torpedo and bomb, mainly by bomb. They hoped to set air against sea, and they believed that air would win. So this attack was inevitable, as others are inevitable. It was the outcome of the German faith in the omnipotence of destruction from the air. And it was mounted in a manner absolutely typical of German war doctrine. First, it was made by aircraft working at short range from a nearby base; secondly it was made in mass. When our fighters went in and tore the first formation to pieces, another, bigger formation was sent out; when that met the same fate, a third and yet bigger was sent out.

It is remarkable - and in some ways revolting - the way these German machine-men will come dumbly on in wave on wave to the slaughter. But, as always, this dumb slavish discipline wilts before thinking, rational, scientific team-work such as our fighter pilots set against it. Now, these three actions were distinct, the first taking place at nine in the morning, the last between four and five in the evening. From their look-out posts in occupied France the Germans had evidently been watching a convoy steaming slowly along the narrow waters of the Channel. They could hardly have had more perfect conditions for their attack. They had bases near, and there were layers of cloud which afforded them excellent cover. There must have seemed to the Germans a good chance of making the bombing raid and getting away before our fighters could reach the scene. But German preparations always take count of all possibilities. So in case our fighters got there, they had a big escort of German fighters flying far above the dive-bombers which were to do the work.

That formation towered up 20,000 feet. It came out on the convoy which had already been harassed by German motor torpedo-boats. The dive-bombers went down on their targets. But our fighters were there in force. And so attack was met by counter-attack. As the bombers went down, our fighters dropped on to them. As the German escort fighters dived to the rescue, other of our fighters, profiting by their superior speed, tackled them. That was the opening stage. Then the battle was free for all. There were many duels. Individual pilots - including a Polish pilot - found and took their opportunities. The aircraft engaged included not only the relatively old Junkers 87 dive-bombers but also the newer Junkers 88 bombers and the new Heinkel 113 fighters. In addition the German force included Messerschmitt 109 single-engined fighters and Messerschmitt 110 twin-engined cannon fighters. So the German formations were representative of the enemy's latest and best aircraft. Our own machines were Spitfires and Hurricanes. Fairly strong forces of them were engaged.

Fighter speeds would have been around the 400 miles an hour mark, and bomber speeds 300.

The fastest aeroplanes in the battle were the Spitfires, but I dare say the Heinkel 113 fighters are not much slower. They are very small machines with a big engine and their speed must be greater than either of the Messerschmitts'.

The Junkers 87 dive-bombers are rather slow and have fixed undercarriages; but the Junkers 88 bombers are capable of more than 300 miles an hour.

And now I want to point to one aspect of these battles which may have importance in the future. It concerns the difficulty of employing aircraft in mass. The Germans, as I have mentioned, rely on the destructive effect of air bombing to close the sea routes around our coasts. But to gain that end, their bombers must be able to work in large numbers. Moreover, when they meet fierce opposition they must have adequate protection or they cannot do their bombing. Now, our aircraft are known to be superior to the German in speed and powers of manoeuvre. They are technically better aeroplanes. But the Germans have greater numbers of aeroplanes. So the Germans must always be pitting their numbers against our technical excellence. And they have been doing that. They've been so arranging their dispositions that, in battle, they nearly always have had numerical superiority.

But the sizes of formations are growing. Now, when a formation is two hundred strong the limit to the numbers which can be effectively controlled in battle by existing systems is being approached.

It is true that new theories for using aircraft in mass have been devised. But most of them depend upon the use of new types of aircraft. They would be impossible to adopt without using new types. So the Germans are approaching the point where their formations are becoming so big as to be unwieldy. That's the point. They are reaching the blundering stage.

If an air formation reaches the clumsy, blundering stage, its size becomes a source of weakness instead of strength. The small, well-drilled, highly proficient formation will cut it to pieces.

Above all things I do not want to be over-optimistic. I spend most of my time trying to counter over-optimistic stories. But it is a fact that the Germans are going to find increasing difficulty in using their vast numbers of aircraft effectively on military targets. Our convoys are protected not only by anti-aircraft guns and balloon barrages - these towed balloon barrages, by the way, are proving very useful - but also by our well-drilled, quick-acting, though relatively small formations of fighters which can be rushed to any scene of action off our coasts at any moment. The Germans will find difficulty in countering the activities of those fighters simply by multiplying the size of their formations. The point we can note now is that huge numbers of aircraft can reach a point when they defeat themselves by becoming unwieldy and uncontrollable. New methods of controlling huge numbers of aircraft effectively have been thought out, but they mostly depend on new types of machines which do not yet exist.

So it seems to be permissible to draw one inference from the Royal Air Force victory. It is that, in their attempts to cut our sea routes by air action, the Germans have so far failed and that they are not likely to succeed any better by throwing much greater numbers of aircraft into the battle. Mass use of aircraft has been the German ideal. Their belief is that mass formations of bombers can wreak such destruction that neither land position can stand up to it. But though mass formations may be easy to handle when there is little opposition, they tend to disintegrate or to become entangled when there is strong opposition. Now here is another inference to be drawn from these attacks on our convoys in the Channel. The attacks are made, as I said at the beginning at short range.

They are made on objectives which the Germans can see from the French coast. In fact the Germans have every possible advantage.

Contrast the problem before the Germans if they wanted to make daylight attacks on objectives well inland. Supposing they wanted to bomb some part of London. Instead of dashing out fifteen or twenty miles from their bases, they would have to go at least eighty miles out and eighty miles back. If our fighters can get at them when they do a twenty miles hit-and-run raid, they would have a better chance of getting at them if they tried an eighty miles raid. I repeat that I think over-optimism is a thing to be guarded against. We know that the Germans have not yet employed their full air strength against us. We know that the numerical strength and the powers of destruction of the German air force are enormous. But if we examine quite calmly and critically that battle off Dover, if we note how close to German occupied territory it was fought, how big were the German losses and how small ours, I think we must conclude that, if the Germans change from ship to land targets and raid Great Britain in force by daylight, the chances are that the Royal Air Force will give them so heavy a blow that it will cripple them.

The Royal Air Force has high on its list of unforgivable sins the major crime of what it calls 'shooting a line' - that is, talking in any heroic sort of way about a job done, or a fight, or in fact, about any of those adventures which are just the things you or I, as outsiders, like to hear and read about. For instance, I know at least one fighter station, which, even in peacetime, had a 'Line book', and pilots who obtained any publicity at all, however innocent, were invited to contribute sums of money to charity by way of penance. I know about that book because, several times before the

A Royal Air Force Supermarine Spitfire trails smoke after attacking a German Heinkel He 111H/P bomber during the Battle of Britain.

war, I went down to that particular aerodrome with a recording car to record impressions of a fighter station at work, and, before I could get any pilot to take part, or to face the microphone, I had to insure him against the cost of the 'Line' he was going to shoot.

Sir Kingsley Wood himself, when he was Secretary of State for Air, summed up this Service attitude when he said to a group of war correspondents in France: "Remember, in the Royal Air Force it is never the individual man who does anything - it is always the R.A.F. which does it." But, being an ordinary individual, who so far hasn't had that Service ideal put into me, I'm afraid that I haven't been able to look at things in quite that light. Whenever I think back on the many glorious things done by the Royal Air Force, particularly that part of the R.A.F. which was in France, I obstinately find myself thinking, not of the Service as a whole, but of the individual pilot. In writing, therefore, it is the deeds of these men which I want to put on record, because, though they may be comparatively unimportant against the enormous and horrible backcloth of war, they do, together, form the glorious pattern of victory.

Turning back the pages of memory, then, we come to the first week of the war. In France, our Fairey Battle bombers had been flying up and down the Siegfried Line, taking photographs, and the Germans had brought up a strong fighter defence of Messerschmitts to keep them away. One morning a Squadron-Leader took off from a large field not far from Reims, at the head of a formation of five Battles. He was going on yet another reconnaissance to the German lines, but, on his way, he was intercepted by twenty enemy fighters. There could only be one end to such a meeting, for the Battles are slow and are defended by only one rear gun. But the Squadron-Leader had an important job to do and he continued towards Germany.

CHAPTER 9

FIRST REAL AIR FIGHT OF THE WAR

T HE FIGHT which followed lasted for quite a long time, and our Battles, although outnumbered and out manoeuvred by the fast German single-seaters, fought their way on towards the Siegfried Line. In the end they went down, one by one, until only the Squadron-Leader remained. Alone he continued the patrol, and, eventually, with his machine shot up till it was hardly holding together, he managed to get back to his aerodrome and make a crash landing. This was the first real air fight of the war, and the first indication of that determination of our pilots to press home the attack - which makes all the difference between them and the pilots of the *Luftwaffe*.

Not long after that I remember another piece of deliberate courage and daring, although, this time, it was not in an actual combat. A Sergeant-Pilot was flying a Hurricane which caught on fire in the air. At the time he was flying low, but he was just high enough to get out safely with his parachute, so he opened the top of his cockpit and prepared to bale out. But, just as he was going to jump, he realised that his blazing machine would almost certainly crash among the houses of a French village just ahead of him, so he got back into his seat again. Then, in spite of the flames, he stuck at the controls and headed the Hurricane out for open country. By that time his machine was down to 400 feet, and when, eventually, he did jump, it was touch and go whether his parachute would open in time. Luckily it did, and he got away with only bruises from his heavy fall. His plane crashed, and blew up with an explosion which would certainly have killed several people had he not risked his life to keep it away from the village.

It was not long after this that the cruel winter of 1939-1940 set in across the whole of Europe, and, in our part of France, there began the spell of bitter cold and snow which lasted for months. It was during this spell that we had the epic of what is now known as 'The Ice Flight.' The first we knew of this was when early one morning a group of flying crews came into our hotel. They were half blue with cold and still in agony from the pain in their feet and their fingers. When they had thawed out and had had some food, we began to piece together the story of their night's adventure. These men had been flying Whitley bombers on a night leaflet raid to Munich and had been 'upstairs' for over seven hours. As soon as they'd taken off they had run into ice-formation, and throughout their whole flight the pilots had had to fight against the layers of ice which formed and re-formed over their wings and their controls. But they flew on, reached Munich, and turned back towards France. By this time the temperature in the cabins themselves was thirty degrees below freezing, and the crews were in such pain that from time to time they had to cry out loud to give themselves some relief. Then, just over our lines, still flying in the pitch darkness, and with the windscreens so frosted over that it was hopeless even to try to look out of them, the Whiteleys began to get out of control. One of them had an engine catch fire and began to go down in a spin. Both the pilots hauled on the stick and on the rudder together and they managed to pull her out, but, in so doing, part of the rudder snapped away. Still unable to see a thing in front of them, and with their machine only just controllable, the pilots managed to put it down on a hillside, where it burnt itself out after the crew had clambered clear. They spent the night sitting warming themselves round the red-hot wreckage. Meanwhile, two more Whitleys had managed to reach their aerodrome, while the crew of another had had to bale out by parachute. All the men who had taken part in the flight eventually gathered at the aerodrome and later flew back to England.

The official communiqué issued on the night's work was impressive by its understatement. It said simply: "More successful reconnaissance flights were carried out by our aircraft last night."

In May, when Hitler invaded the Low Countries, our Advanced

Air Striking Force immediately became the main air weapon against the hordes of his tanks pouring through the Sedan gap. It is now no secret that all the dirty jobs came the way of our squadrons-the bombing of those treacherously open bridges over the Meuse; the closing of strategic roads; attacks against heavily defended supply columns and bases; and, above all, attacks against overwhelming numbers of German aircraft.

I remember going up to one of our bomber aerodromes on the second or third day of the blitzkrieg. There I found a Flight-Lieutenant friend of mine looking very worried and carrying around a sheaf of orders. He waved them about and said to me: 'orders to bomb this and bomb that and bomb the other, but for heaven's sake-what with? Every machine we ever had is out, and has been all day, except for refuelling and bombing up.'

That remark, more than any other I can think of, describes how the Advanced Air Striking Force was working. Every time they went out they were chased and chivvied round the sky by Messerschmitt's and by AA fire. But as soon as they landed from one show, they were getting ready to take off on the next, and some of them even wandered off in little parties of their own. There was one Canadian pilot who always had the habit of coming back about a quarter of an hour or so after the rest of his flight. He never volunteered very much explanation for this, but his combat reports showed that, not content with doing his bombing, he had gone off searching for troop concentrations, and had flown up and down machine-gunning them. Actually, just after one of these raids, I managed to get permission for this pilot to record a broadcast for me, and we got so far as preparing the script and getting it passed by the censor. When we got up to the aerodrome with the recording car, however, we were just in time to see him taking off on an emergency job, and, as soon as he landed again, he had to go off on something else, so we never got that broadcast.

The work done by the original Fighter squadrons of the A.A.S.F., and, later, by the other squadrons which came up to reinforce them, would fill a whole book - and, doubtless, in the fullness of time will do so. I used to see those Hurricane pilots most evenings during the blitzkrieg, when they came into our town after dusk to get a bath, which they found was the most refreshing thing they could get after a day's work. They were always dog-tired, half asleep, dirty, and unshaven but yet always somehow cheery, and their table in the restaurant was always the noisiest and most hilarious of the lot. There was not a man among them who hadn't shot down more than one German - and many of them, like 'Cobber' Kain and Orton (who incidentally has just got the Bar for his D.F.C.) and 'Ginger' Paul, have long since got into double figures.

At one time it was said that this famous flight of three machines flown by Kain, Orton, and Paul had accounted for seventy Germans. These boys, all in their early twenties, spend day after day fighting against odds of ten, twenty, and thirty to one, and yet somehow they always managed to get back. One night, we would see Kain and Paul come in and would ask, rather hesitatingly, what had happened to Orton. The answer would come: 'Oh, he's all right; he baled out our side of the lines and I expect he'll be along soon.' Half an hour later there would be a yell from the other side of the room, and in would walk Orton, clamouring for dinner. The next night it might be Paul who was missing - but somehow the full flight always turned up in the end, and those three stuck together until Paul and Orton went home. It was not long after this that Kain, who was due to go home the very next day, killed himself in a flying accident on his own aerodrome.

Individual acts of heroism during the blitzkrieg are far too numerous to mention. There was the famous bombing of the Meuse bridges by five volunteer pilots, only one of whom returned. The leaders of this flight, Flying-Officer Garland and Sergeant Gray, were awarded the first air V.C.s of the war. Then there was the severely wounded bomber pilot who swam the River Meuse to escape and to bring home valuable information. There was, too, case after case of British fighter pilots going straight to the attack against odds of twenty to one, and it was this courage and resolution which paved the way for our air supremacy at Dunkirk. The Germans by then had had a taste of the individual merits of our men and machines, and there can be little doubt that the enemy morale had been badly shaken.

It is because of the things that I set down here, and because of other deeds equally brave, that I am sure the local supremacy at Dunkirk will remain with us in the fight for the English Channel and for Britain.

Already we have seen that the fighters of the Royal Air Force have been improving on their first figure of four to one. On Sunday, July 14 I was able to stand on the cliffs of Dover and watch a German attempt to bomb a convoy about a mile off-shore.

A few minutes later we saw about twenty Junkers-87 dive-bombers coming from the direction of Calais at about 6,000 feet, and above them was an escort of about the same number of Messerschmitt's. Lewis immediately started up the recording gear and Phillips and I took the microphone out, to watch. The Germans started a chain-bombing attack on the convoy, and there was a terrific din of AA fire all round and from the ships themselves. Our first record got the crash of a number of bombs and the bangs of the AA guns, together with my commentary, and we had the luck to see a Junkers shot down straight into the sea in front of us. Then the German bombers turned for home, and a series of dog-fights broke out all round us between the Messerschmitt's, Hurricanes, and Spitfires. These were very difficult to follow, but we were able to describe some of them and to see two more German machines crash. During the action Lewis managed to change his cutter needle twice without causing any appreciable break in the recording.

As soon as the battle was over we rang up the BBC and told them that we were on our way back. Censors were good enough to come straight away to Broadcasting House to pass the records, and just over an hour after our return they were being broadcast.

But to get back to my original point - what I saw of this action was enough to convince me that the Germans have great respect for our defences. The Junkers never ventured close in-shore and the Messerschmitt's only stopped long enough to see several of their number shot down, before they turned for home. In all, the enemy lost seven machines that afternoon, while we lost only one. The damage done to the convoy was slight, and the German claim afterwards that four merchant ships, a destroyer, and an armed auxiliary cruiser had been badly hit and set on fire is as ridiculous as their statement that they lost only two machines.

Manning the rear turret of a Wellington heavy bomber is like sitting in space with a couple of machine-guns in front of you. Looking dead astern with the turret in its normal position, one can see nothing except the sky; not even the tail-plane can be seen, for the turret is behind it. One feels entirely isolated from the rest of the crew, and, indeed, from the rest of the aircraft; it is just as though the bomber were towing the turret. For a person who likes solitude the rear-gunner's job is the ideal occupation. Coming from the other end of the aircraft - almost like voices from another machine - the gunner can hear conversation between the captain and the navigator, the observer, and the wireless operator. Though he, too, can speak to the others through the inter-communication system, a talkative man 'in the tail' is regarded, quite rightly, as a nuisance. In the ordinary way, therefore, he has anything from four to eight hours ahead of him for the enjoyment of his own society.

The tail-gunner's job is to keep an unceasing watch over the entire area within his view to the rear of the aircraft (and from the turret he has a splendid field of vision); to report any incident such as anti-aircraft fire from the ground, and to take immediate action to deal with any hostile attack.

When the tail-gunner enters the turret at the beginning of a raid, this is his normal procedure after the bomber has taken off. First he puts his parachute handy, locks the turret doors, and prepares for action. He rotates his turret to see that it is moving freely; sees to his guns and sights, his lighting system and spare bulbs, and checks his reserve ammunition. He plugs in on his inter-communication set and speaks to the captain; then he settles down to keep watch, marking each section of the sky to right and left, above and below, just as if it were a sector of the countryside.

Once he is clear of the English coast he asks permission to fire a short burst to try his guns. Soon the aircraft will be over enemy or enemy-occupied territory where enemy fighters may be met, though in point of fact they seldom trouble the bombers at night. Some of the more enthusiastic men in our night bombing squadrons are in consequence beginning to complain that they don't get enough to do. Still, if orders permit they may get the opportunity of strafing a ground target.

But the big moment - the moment for which all the rear-gunner's training has prepared him and in which the rest of the crew will depend upon him - comes when an attacking aircraft approaches within range of his powerful Browning guns. If the bomber is flying alone the rear-gunner will have to deal with the attack himself if it is made from the stern; when a number of bombers are flying in formation any attackers would have to meet their concentrated fire.

In the early months if an aircraft changed direction it would be 30 seconds or so before the people on the ground would know that it had done so; and they did not know whether it had gone up or down, or right or left. By the time they had realised that it had changed its direction, it might be anything up to two miles away from where they thought it was. That is why searchlights used to wave apparently aimlessly about in the skies. They were looking on an arc which would bring them across the path of the aircraft whichever way he had turned. It was very confusing to our fighters and they disliked it intensely. We have changed all that now.

Searchlights are now able to help the night-fighters. They indicate to them the present position and course of the enemy aircraft. Incidentally, it is not uncommon for an aircraft to be illuminated as seen by the fighter pilot while from the ground it is invisible.

Searchlights are exposed under the orders of Fighter Command or their lower formation headquarters; in order to make sure that co-operation is perfect.

There are other, less commonly known, jobs done by searchlights. They expose their lights to direct home our own aircraft which are lost. As many as 30 aircraft and more have been successfully "homed" in a single night. These incidents run to pattern rather as follows.

It was raining and misty when Gunner Laurence Smith, aged 28, turned out at 5.15 a.m. for duty. Smith, a grocery shop manager until a year before, was still rather sleepy when, nearly two hours later, he heard the faint drone of a British bomber. The clouds were low, the drizzle had given way to heavy storm. As Gunner Smith listened, he detected that the bomber's engines were not running well and guessed that the pilot had lost his way although he was only ten miles from his base. When the bomber came low, Gunner Smith put a beam on it, then flashed the beam across to the bomber's base. He repeated that manoeuvre several times until the pilot realised he was being shown the way home. The pilot took the tip, followed the beam across country and landed safely. Another bomber which was also lost followed him in. Not long afterwards messages were sent out asking for the name of the man who had shown such initiative in putting on the beam during daylight. Pilots and crews of both bombers wanted to say "thank you" to Gunner Smith for acting as their guide and probably saving them and the machines.

- C H A P T E R   1 0 -

THE SEARCHLIGHTS

THE SEARCHLIGHTS watch the sea. If a man bales out over the channel there is a most complete system of communication, and-intelligence can be passed in a matter of minutes right round to Fighter Command and back again to the rescue parties. If a pilot is seen baling out the word goes round and the rescue launch is sent off at once. It is very much quicker than if it had to be done by local police, who must send their reports through the telephone exchanges.

On one occasion four airmen were reported to be some miles out at sea in a dinghy after their bomber had crashed, but their actual position was not known. The searchlights played on the sea and a Bombardier in charge of the searchlights was the first to sight the dinghy. It was about two miles away. It was held in the light and at first seemed to be drifting towards the shore, but the men were huddled together and in danger of being swamped. A heavy sea was running and it was obvious that the rescue would take some time. But, guided by the light, rescue craft headed towards the dinghy, and at last a corvette steamed into the beam. The four airmen were then picked up and returned to a base.

In a similar way, searchlights in the neighbourhood of balloon barrages must be prepared at any time to illuminate balloons if it appears that our own aircraft are in danger of flying into them. This danger frequently occurs and has frequently been averted.

Searchlight sites are equipped with light machine guns for action against low-flying aircraft. They have shot down many enemy 'planes. Here is a personal account by L-Bombardier Hanson who shot down a plane on May 10th, 1941.

"Just after midnight we exposed the beam and a few minutes later a 'plane swooped out of the clouds. It was flying very low… it couldn't have been much more than 100 feet… and we saw at once that it was a Jerry. The Sergeant in charge immediately ordered us to disperse the beam (that's to dazzle the pilot) and ordered machine-gun action. I'd been waiting for that moment for fifteen weary months… and I was almost petrified at my luck. The Heinkel didn't seem to be in any difficulties, and as I opened tire I couldn't help wondering why he didn't have a go at us, either with a bomb or a machine gun. After a few rounds the Lewis gun jammed, but we put that right and blazed away again. Then Jerry flew away and we instantly had to engage two more targets with the beam. Ten minutes later, when we'd practically forgotten him, the Heinkel flew back and circled over the site like a giant bat. I didn't have time to think ... all I remember saying to myself is 'Well, I've been wanting action. Lad, you're going to have a basinful now.' I blazed away and every rifle on the site was being fired in support. After two or three minutes the Heinkel flew away again, but five minutes later it was back for the third time.

'By the fourth time we were getting a bit irritated. The Jerry 'plan' was like: mosquito at a picnic. You just couldn't brush the darned thing away. But this time was K.O. The 'plane crashed in a nearby field and burst into flames as it hit the ground. A party was detailed to go to the 'plane and there we found three of the crew dead. The pilot, who had a machine-gun bullet in his head, wore the Iron Cross. The fourth member of the crew - I think he was a wireless operator - was staggering about with a bullet in his leg and was obviously dazed and in great pain. Yes, it was a swell night. The only fellow who was a bit glum about the whole affair was my mate, whose night off it was. If it had been the next night, he'd have landed the Jerry instead of me."

Searchlights also mark the mines which fall in the Thames and other places. They mark them scientifically by taking the bearing. This, of course, speeds the minesweepers' work and to a certain extent reduces their risks. It saves a lot of time and a number of ships.

- C H A P T E R   1 1 -

IT WAS A FINE VISIT

I T WAS a fine evening with a dull sky to the north. About 10.30 p.m. the traces of two unidentified aircraft were picked up by a gun operations room in east Scotland. They were plotted as approaching the coast from the south of the Faroe Islands. As they neared land they separated, one turning north and the other continuing overland in a westerly direction. The 'plane which turned north was soon identified as a friendly one. The other was presumably hostile.

The raider was again plotted flying due west to the south of Moffat at a height of 5,000 feet, and again south of Cambuslang. Then the plotting stopped near Busby and all trace was lost.

All gun and searchlight sites were standing by, for the 'plane was getting dangerously near Glasgow. At 11 p.m. the spotter on a searchlight site about eight miles south of the city saw a 'plane clearly in the moonlight. He immediately identified it as a Me.110. The warning was flashed to the heavy guns at Glasgow. On every searchlight site the Lewis gunner gripped his butt a little tighter in the hope that he might get in a burst at the enemy.

At 11.07 p.m. a neighbouring site again caught a glimpse of the plane still flying west. As they watched, it turned and began to circle the site. The pilot seemed to be checking his position. Twice it circled round the site. The air was quiet, the pilot had switched off his engine: and then, to everybody's consternation, he took a shallow dive straight at the site. From the 'plane a parachute streamed out. Some thought, with subsequently growing conviction, that they had seen a man silhouetted against the moonlight as he baled out. Others thought they were being dive-bombed. All thought their last moment had come, but just when the 'plane about to strike the site it turned off, crashed to the ground not 250 yards away and burst into flames. This was the telephonist's great moment. He proudly reported the affair to headquarters while the detachment formed two parties, one to attend to the burning 'plane, the other to hunt the parachutist.

Meanwhile, two AA signalmen, hearing the crashing 'plane, had come running out of their quarters in time to see the pilot floating slowly to earth. Half-dressed, they rushed towards the place where they knew there was a small farmhouse. When they reached it, the back door opened and a ploughman appeared.

"Are you looking for a parachutist?" he inquired.

They said they were.

"Well, he's inside now, arrived about half a minute ago," said the ploughman.

They dashed into the cottage.

There in an armchair, dressed in a fleece-lined brown leather-flying suit, sat the parachutist. He threw out his hands to prove they were empty, and said, "Ah! British soldiers - no guns - no bombs." They immediately searched him for weapons, but found none. The prisoner also said that his 'plane was unarmed. They asked his name. "Alfred Horn," he replied: and as they couldn't understand him properly he wrote it down on a piece of paper.

"Where have you come from?" they asked him. He replied, "Munich in four hours."

One of the soldiers went to telephone headquarters for a car to remove "Alfred Horn," whose ankle was apparently injured by his fall. The other soldier looked curiously at the prisoner, for he had heard much about the poor quality of German clothes. There was nothing of this in the clothing "Horn" wore. His fleece-lined suit and boots were of good leather. He wore a gold wristwatch, and carried what looked like a Leica camera round his neck. A map with his course roughly plotted was strapped round his knee.

He asked if he might keep his parachute as a souvenir. The soldier gave a non-committal reply and asked him if he had ever been to England before. "No," he replied; and after a pause, "I have a very important message for the Duke of Hamilton," whom he said he had met at the Berlin Olympic Games. He seemed to want to be friendly, and showed them a picture of his wife and son with whom he said he had spent that morning. One of the soldiers asked him if he would like to return to Germany if he got the chance. He immediately shouted, "No! No! No! No!"

The scene where the 'plane had crashed was increasingly confused. There were policemen, the Fire Brigade, the A.F.S., the Home Guard, soldiers from neighbouring units, R.A.F. men and many civilians. The searchlight detachment were ordered to fix bayonets, and even then had great difficulty in clearing the field. Many pieces of the 'plane had disappeared into the cars in which spectators had arrived, but these were eventually all recovered and handed over. Its machine guns were brand new. There was no ammunition, and the gun barrels were filled up with grease.

One of the gunners, on return from escorting the prisoner, had a strong idea that he had seen a photograph of him recently. Every newspaper and magazine to hand were diligently scanned, and suddenly the gunner shouted, "That's him! I'm sure that's him!" He pointed to a photograph of a dark, strongly built man, a Nazi, with thick black hair and deep-set eyes. It was a photograph of Rudolf Hess, Hitler's Deputy. How they all laughed.

Their troop officer had been sent to the Home Guard headquarters, where an R.A.F. Intelligence Officer was interrogating the prisoner, assisted by a crowd of officers and others. The contents of the prisoner's pockets were emptied out on to the desk, including two hypodermic syringes, a phial of liquid and two bottles of white tablets. The troop officer turned to the R.A.F. officer who was at the moment doing the interrogating, and said:

'You know, sir, I believe this is Rudolf Hess. I've seen him in Germany, and I recognise him as Hess."

'Don't be a fool," he was told.

He wasn't being.

CHAPTER 12

THE PILOTS THAT TOOK PART

T HE ROYAL Air Force drew its pilots from a number of sources. As well as the regulars, and those on short service commissions from Britain and the commonwealth countries there were others that formed the University Air Squadrons as well as the auxiliaries.

During the early part of the Battle of Britain, Royal Air Force relied mostly on the reservists and the part time flyers who were the mainstay of Fighter Command. Most were either young, 'green' and under trained or had been with the R.A.F. for so long that they were actually past their peak, although if we look at the records we would find that many of the 'aces' were actually over thirty years of age. The cream of the British fighter pilots for some reason were transferred to Bomber Command between the two world wars and at the outbreak of the Second World War it left Fighter Command in a rather dilapidated position.

Often we are accustomed to seeing the fighter pilot in silk lined flying jackets with silk scarves bellowing in the wind as they race around in their open wheeler two seater sports cars and with their public school education throw out remarks like "I say old chap, did you enjoy that pancake with the Spit?". News and film media have always displayed the role of the fighter pilot in this fashion, but actually out of the 3,500 Fighter Command pilots that took part in the Battle of Britain, only about 200 had received a public school education. 601 Squadron had a number of these, and the parking lot at Tangmere used to look like a starting point for a 'concours de elegance' with brightly coloured MG's and Austin Healey's looking in far better shape than the Hurricanes that they flew. It has been said that these pilots actually bought the local service station so as to keep their cars on the road. Most of the pilots came from much humbler backgrounds, there were bank clerks, young doctors, factory workers, shop assistants and hundreds who had just ordinary jobs. Many of these were given a hard time by the educated contingent and quite a bit of resentment followed. So do not be fooled into believing that most Fighter Command pilots spoke in university and educated fashion as many movies depict as most of them came from just ordinary backgrounds. But, they did, as other branches of the services had, a certain form of sayings and terminology spoken within the R.A.F.:

Pilots were called up to serve in the R.A.F. in a number of ways, many applied to serve with the Royal Air Force after seeing the many recruitment posters displayed all over Britain. Quite a few were already serving with the R.A.F. while others already belonged to University Air Squadrons such as Oxford, Cambridge and London, and Eton although only a school, was very well represented with many Etonians going to the other University Air Squadrons. Many, after having part time training belonged to the Auxiliary Air Force and these pilots were given 'Calling Out Papers' like the one shown above that was issued

British pilot Barrie Heath of No. 611 Squadron R.A.F. posing with his Spitfire fighter, 1940.

to 'Sandy' Johnstone who was directed to report to 602 City of Glasgow Squadron. Another was Australian born Pilot Officer Richard Hillary who attended Oxford University who went to 603 "City of Edinburgh" Squadron. Many of these pilots flying for the first time together were sent to France, some immediately became heroes like Edgar 'Cobber' Kain a New Zealander who claimed his first Dornier Do17 in November 1939, then shot down another Do17 just fifteen days later. 'Cobber' chalked up 17 confirmed victories before being killed in an accident in June 1940. He was awarded the DFC.

"Funny this was, although I worked in banking, I had applied to get into the RCAF but it appeared that they didn't want me. With the war just started in England, I felt that I had a chance over there.

"At the time the R.A.F. were taking just about anybody they could get their hands on. They had a terrific shortage of pilots, I think half of the pilots were from the Commonwealth, a lot of us were Canadians. I applied, I got called up on a Monday, had the medical on Wednesday and sailed for England on the Friday."

Pilot Officer Alfred Keith Ogilvie 609 Squadron R.A.F.

Prior to 1939 when the possibility of war could become a reality, Britain arranged for short service commissions where pilots that had already received basic and fundamental training, could further their experience with flying and combat skills. A number of pilots that undertook this scheme came from Canada and Australia. Many Australian airmen were trained at the R.A.A.F. Training School at Point Cook in Victoria, and many took advantage of the offer of a short service commission with the R.A.F.. Many others applied for enrolment into the Empire Training Scheme and commenced their training in Canada. It was here that they had the opportunity of selecting whether they wanted to go into Fighter, Bomber or Coastal Command. An Australian was asked what he would like to be, and he answered, "I'll be a gunner", to which the desk clerk said "Why do you want to become a gunner?" "All right, I'll be a navigator then" to which the desk clerk politely asked "Why do you want to be a navigator?" So the Australian said "Then I'll be a pilot if that's all right with you." And that's what the Australian got, he saw the war through as a bomber pilot.

Many pilots recorded victories, but in general, most pilots complained of the condition of the aircraft saying that they were, in conjunction with the inexperience of the new pilots, no match for the *Luftwaffe* pilots who already had considerable combat experience.

"Look, you've got to face it, France was a shambles. Everyone tried their best, but most of us pilots were not only new to flying in combat, we were new to flying in general. If an Me. was coming towards you firing all guns, you would push the stick forward, your heart seems to go up into your throat as he flies past you. You know he's going to make a tight turn, the Me. was like that, and your ticker would be pounding nine to the dozen as you looked in the mirror, looked from side to side but couldn't see him, but you knew he was there, instinct told you he was there. For the new pilot it was panic stations, okay, we were told not to panic, but it was human nature. We learnt by those mistakes, your leader might call out over the radio that the 'hun' was on your tail calling you by your code name, but in a state of panic, it was not unusual to even forget what your code name was." - Sgt G.C.Bennett 609 Squadron. (Later killed in 1941)

The conditions in France were backed up by many.

"We were ordered to attack the advancing German columns around Sedan. On the 11th and 12th May, everybody got back all right. Then on the 13th May five of our aircraft went again on exactly the same course for the third day running. Only one came back. After that it was chaos. We did some leaflet dropping at night. Those of us who were left moved from field to field, half a dozen times a fortnight. A lot of people just got lost. We ended up with two other Battles from Squadrons we did not know, alone in a field somewhere in Central France... Our aircraft was had been damaged a good bit by then, but we found another that was missing a tail wheel, we put our tail wheel on it, pushed the ground crew in the back, and took off. All I had was a cycling map of Northern France." - Sgt. Arthur Power 88 'Battle' Squadron

As time progressed, many friendships blossomed between the educated and the ordinary bloke. Soon all were to realize that they were out there to do a job, and that was to become the master of the plane that they were flying and move in on the 'Hun' for the kill. As news came in telling them that someone had not returned, or was missing or killed in action, they felt as though they had lost a member of their family, but it was the courage of the fighter pilot that he would immediately go down to the pub as if nothing had happened.

"It was hard when word came in that one of your mates was missing, another pilot may have given a graphic account of how he saw someone go down in flames and hadn't a chance to bale out. You sort of somehow found a big hole in your stomach momentarily. But you could not afford to think of such matters, you put your mind to other things, you got drunk or whatever. You train yourself to think of only one thing, and that is the job that lies ahead." - George Barclay 151 Squadron.

"We were all amateurs. Yet the young pilots lived their lives to the full because they knew that any day they'd be dead." - Gregory Kirkorian. R.A.F. Squadron Intelligence.

"The waiting was the worst part, we'd sit around playing poker with that tension pit in our stomachs - it was almost a relief when we heard the phone ring to scramble." - Group Captain Peter Matthews.

Life was not easy for the fighter pilot, every day was a long day, generally up before dawn making preparations for the day that lay ahead. Some days he was on the go from before dawn to well after the sun had gone down. He had to contend with squadron mates who failed to return, maybe missing in action or as was the usual story, killed in the line of duty. No one knew what the next day was to bring, most although were intent on claiming victory over the enemy, they were in fact just fighting for survival, they drank to lost loved ones then prayed for their own safety.

And why did they do it? According to P/O H.G. Niven, "All you wanted to do was to fly, we were young and had no real moral angle, you wanted action because you were twenty or so, you could fly, you knew how to fly and you knew you had to fly because there was a war on." But whether or not your prayers would be answered, those that died as well as those who survived were duly recognized after the war by being able to display a rosette and clasp on their 1939-45 star indicating that they, as pilots of Fighter Command took place in the greatest battle of all time, "The Battle of Britain."

It was a different story with the *Luftwaffe*. These pilots had received exceptional training, and Germany was producing some 800 trained pilots a month compared with only 200 a month in the R.A.F.. Not only that, the *Luftwaffe* pilots were combat trained having seen action in such places as Spain, Poland, Norway and Belgium.

The *Luftwaffe* had a comprehensive training program and with so many experienced pilots they helped and assisted any of the new pilots assigned to their squadrons. Relations between the officers of the *Luftwaffe* and the junior ranks were far superior than that of the R.A.F. and the morale of the men was greater as well. It was back in 1923 that the *Reichswehr-Ministerium* (The German Defence Ministry) signed an agreement with the Soviet Union that allowed them to set up complete training facilities near Lipezk. Pilots, observers and aircraft mechanics were sent there to undertake a thorough and complete schedule of training. With others being trained at the Deutscher Luftsport-Verband which was a sporting flying club, most of the *Luftwaffe* personnel were experience men during the period with the Legion Kondor during the Spanish Civil War, then later in the conflicts in Norway, Belgium, Holland and in France.

Before and during the early part of the second world war, all

German aircrew had to undergo at least six months basic training, and keeping in line with the strong Nazi belief in physical training, this included drill, various forms of sport and light and gymnastics. In the classroom they were taught the fundamentals of flight and aerodynamics, navigation and the laws of aviation. Prior to the outbreak of war, the Germans practiced their flying skills in aircraft that was not visually designed as military aircraft in keeping with the restrictions imposed on them by the Treaty of Versailles way back in 1919, but closer inspection of the aircraft revealed a very strong military influence. Later more military style aircraft, advanced aircraft skills and learnt more about combat defence and attacking tactics before they were given their licence. Those that were training as bomber crews were transferred to another school where another 60-80 hours were spent undergoing intense training on more advanced aircraft and then to specialist training on instrument flying and skills. Once they had practiced simulation sorties on combat operational aircraft, they were ready to join a *Kampfgeschwader* (Bomber Unit). Potential fighter pilots also went further additional advanced training and were sent on to mock air battles before passing out and being allowed to a *Jaggeschwader* (Fighter Unit).

"We were idealists with the honour of being part of the most elite fighting force in the world," said a young aircrew cadet as along with 3,000 others they were addressed by Adolf Hitler on their graduation day in the capital Berlin. "We listen to the spell binding words of our leader and accept them with all our hearts. Never before have we experienced such a deep sense of patriotic devotion towards our beloved German fatherland. I shall never, never forget the expressions of rapture which I saw on the faces around me today."

But even the young *Luftwaffe* pilots admitted that their early combat duties often disclosed their inexperience. A young pilot, on one of his very early combat missions came under attack from R.A.F. fighters:

"It was the first time I had experienced this, it was a kind of ticky, ticky, tick… but it made me feel good that it had protected me. Anyway, what I did was evade whoever was firing at me by nose-diving. Now, I thought, I've got rid of it, so I climbed up again trying to catch up with the unit. I remember thinking, Well, this isn't so bad… The protection had held… but I was still climbing and suddenly there was a second attack from behind. It was so fast that I couldn't evade before it came… at least, I as a beginner couldn't. Suddenly he was there and immediately I went down again. While I was diving I thought, Well, what do I do now?

"Some pilots said that in such a case you just go down to tree-top level and go home… but I thought, Well, that sounds too easy, so I decided to climb up again… which was a big mistake that an experienced man would not have made.

"Then as I was climbing again suddenly I was attacked from below to the right-hand side. Someone who was more at home playing these games had come from below from the right-hand side. In this area there was no protective armour so it was a real problem.

"The glass from the cockpit was splintering, the instrument panel splattered and now I was really hit… or many hits. Somehow at that point I blacked out.

"When I came to I found myself in a vertical dive and what I noticed was lots of noise, a kind of fluid coming from the side of the plane and what struck me was that the ground was approaching very fast. I realized that I had to catch the plane immediately and get it out of the dive. I did and in doing so my blood rushed from my head and I blacked out again. When I came to I found I was at tree-top level with little power left in the machine. It could still fly but with no power. I was now very, very low and had to look for somewhere to land.

"At this stage I looked around and found that there were two Spitfires behind me and they were shooting occasionally, but I guess it was difficult to shoot at me because I was going so slow and was not flying in a straight line. I don't know whether they didn't shoot me because they saw I was in a difficult situation… anyway, I just saw an English park-like landscape, some bushes and trees. There was a group of trees ahead of me and I said to myself, Well, gee, what I have to do is to try to get enough speed by flying directly at the trees and then hope that I have enough speed to jump over them and then go down. I did this and then blacked out once more." - Bruno Petrenko ex Bf109 pilot.

German pilots generally had far more training than the British, even during the period of war; *Luftwaffe* training was intense, where the R.A.F. just could not get their pilots into the air quick enough. The reason for this was that the R.A.F. had a shortage of pilots and aircraft. If you had a months training, then you were one of the lucky ones. A few weeks learning the eliminatory physics of flying at a desk, usually up to about 15-20 hours actual flying, and you were posted. Most learnt the best way (sometimes not the correct way) to fly and be successful was the actual experience gained in combat flying. But flying was only one part, evasion tactics in combat was another, and a "good pilot" you had to be a good shot to shoot down one of the enemy and evade being shot at yourself, and this was not always that easy.

"We learned tactics pretty quickly, but there wasn't much time during the Battle. We learned to spread the vics. One chap was put in as 'weaver' - arse-end Charlie - weaving about behind our formation, keeping look-out. They were often shot down, weaving behind and never seen again.

Sailor Malan was the best pilot of the war, a good tactician; above average pilot and an excellent shot. In the end it comes down to being able to shoot. I was an above average pilot, but not a good shot, so the only way I could succeed was to get closer than the next chap. This wasn't easy Johnny Johnson was a pretty good, average pilot, but an excellent shot.

The answer was that there were was no really successful shooting parameter above 5 degree deflection. Most kills were from behind, coming down on the enemy, or head-on, or in 5 degrees deflection.

The Spitfires guns were harmonized to about 450 yards, but this was spread too far across. Sailor Malan trimmed his own guns down to 200-250 yards, and we all followed suit.

At the end of the day, you had to have luck, and I had my share. Once I had my watch shot off my wrist. It was my own watch, and the Air Ministry wouldn't pay me back for it! Another had a bullet hit his headphones. His ear was a bit of a mess, but at least he was alive."

Air Commodore Alan Deere CBE. DSO. DFC. ex 54 Sqn, 602 Sqn and 611 Sqn R.A.F.

Trimming your guns down to 200-250 yards, not easy, but effective if not daring. And you must remember that the Spitfire was travelling at over 300 mph and that 200 yards would be covered in just a matter of seconds. There again, many experienced pilots trimmed their guns down to even less and others opened fire exceptionally close to their targets.

Squadrons of Royal Air Force Fighter Command were made up of a variety of types. As well as the regular squadrons, there were the voluntary squadrons, the auxiliary squadrons, the Fighter Interception Unit and some Fleet Air Arm units.

The majority of the pilots were of British nationality although it has now been found that many pilots from commonwealth countries, because they carried British passports and not one from their own country were classified as British. Canada immediately responded by sending many pilots, but Australia and New Zealand did not officially make any contribution of pilots. Only those pilots that were serving on short service commissions with the Royal Air Force from Australia and New Zealand were to fight during the Battle of Britain and represented their respective countries.

The United States, because President Roosevelt was campaigning for re-election of the presidency would not get involved with the war in Europe despite many pleas from British

Prime Minister Winston Churchill. The American government also would not sanction any American citizen going to Britain to fight the war in Europe. Seven men however defied United States law and each of them made their way to Britain to join the Royal Air Force and fight in the Battle of Britain.

With the fall of various countries in Europe, many experienced pilots from the air forces of Czechoslovakia, Belgium and Poland made their own ways, many under very difficult circumstances in an effort to get to Britain and join the Royal Air Force. Because of the number of pilots that had made their way from their invaded countries to Britain, the R.A.F. was able to establish individual squadrons such as the 303 Polish and 310 Czech squadrons. Canada was also given their own squadron which was 401 Squadron that originally was 1RCAF Squadron but was renumbered so as to avoid confusion with 1 Squadron R.A.F.. Australia, New Zealand, United States and Belgium did not have their own units during the Battle of Britain but later in the war all these countries were to have their own squadrons.

DIRECTIVE OF AUGUST 15TH 1940 ISSUED BY GÖRING TO ALL LUFTWAFFE COMMANDERS

1. The fighter escort defences of our Stuka formations must be readjusted, as the enemy is concentrating his fighters against our Stuka operations. It appears necessary to allocate three fighter Gruppen to each Stuka Gruppe, one of these fighter Gruppen remains with the Stukas, and dives with them to the attack; the second flies ahead over the target at medium altitude and engages the fighter defences; the third protects the whole attack from above. It will also be necessary to escort Stukas returning from the attack over the Channel.

2. Night attacks on shipping targets are only fruitful when the night is so clear that careful aim can be taken.

3. More importance must be attached to co-operation are not to be broken up except in cases of utmost urgency.

4. The incident of VILGI on August 13 shows that certain unit commanders have not yet learnt the importance of clear orders.

5. I have repeatedly given orders that twin-engined fighters are only to be employed where the range of other fighters is inadequate, or where it is for the purpose of assisting our single-engined aircraft to break off combat.

   Our stocks of twin-engined fighters are not great, and we must use them as economically as possible.

6. Until further orders, operations are to be directed exclusively against the enemy Air Force, including the targets of the enemy aircraft industry allocated to the different *Luftflotten*. Shipping targets, and particularly large naval vessels, are only to be attacked where circumstances are especially propitious. For the moment, other targets should be ignored. We must concentrate our efforts on the destruction of the enemy Air Forces. Our night attacks are essentially dislocation raids, made so that the enemy defences and population shall be allowed no respite. Even these, however, should where possible be directed against Air Force targets.

7. My orders regarding the carrying out of attacks by single aircraft under cover of cloud conditions have apparently not been correctly understood. Where on one afternoon 50 aircraft are despatched without adequate preparation on individual missions, it is probable that the operation will be unsuccessful and very costly. I therefore repeat that such sorties are to be undertaken only by specially selected volunteer crews, who have made a prolonged and intensive study of the target, the most suitable method of attack, and the particular navigational problems involved. By no means all our crews are qualified to undertake such tasks.

8. KGr100 (bombers) is also in future to operate against the enemy Air Force and aircraft industry.

9. It is doubtful if there is any point in continuing the attacks on radar sites, in view of the fact that not one of those attacked has so far been put out of operation.

10. The systematic designation of alternative targets would appear frequently to lead to certain targets being attacked which have absolutely no connection with our strategic aims. It must therefore be achieved that even alternative targets are of importance in the battle against the enemy Air Force.

11. The Commanders-in-Chief of the *Luftflotten* are to report to me on the question of the warnings to be given during enemy air penetrations over the Reich. At present, the warnings are causing a loss of output whose consequences are far graver than those caused by the actual bomb damage. In addition, the frequent air raid warnings are leading to nervousness and strain among the population of Western Germany. On the other hand, we must take into account the risk of heavy loss of life should an attack be launched before a warning has been given.

REICHSMARSCHALL HERMANN GORING
KARINHALL, AUGUST 15, 1940

CHAPTER 13

THE BLITZES ON THE HUMBER

NOW FOR an account in perspective of events and results in a typical area. It should be emphasised that the only reason why Hull was chosen for this analysis is that it is as good an area as any other. There are plenty of areas which would have suited the purpose equally well, and there is no suggestion that the defenders of Hull have worked to any better purpose than people in other parts of the country.

In peace-time Hull ranked as "the Third Port and the Ninth City of the British Isles." Add the war activities - sea, air and land - of the Humber area, and it becomes a very likely target for the *Luftwaffe*. Look at its geographical position and it appears to be a fine training target for learner pilots on their early long-range bombing flights. The result is twofold. The tough Yorkshiremen who live there have had more than their share of raids - say a hundred a year - bombing or merely passing over: while A.D.G.B. Units on the Humber earn the envy of their neighbours who are less frequently in action.

The bulk of the defence has fallen on Yorkshire H.A.A. Regiments. The Searchlight Regiment, which has provided most of the lighting, and a L.A.A. Regiment of Lincolnshire origin have not been without effect in the defence.

The first three months of the war saw very little enemy activity, the first H.A.A. round fired in anger being appropriately on November 5th, 1939, at a low-flying Dornier which escaped. On November 22nd came the first of many mine-layers; this one impertinently settled on the water and machine-gunned the coast-defence site before flying home. Mine-laying and rather aimless bombing, occasionally directed at searchlights, started and grew during this winter and the spring of 1940. March saw the first raids on Hull itself, during one of which A.R.P. Headquarters were devastated by a direct hit, but were in action again within half an hour in a new building. The summer and autumn, so full of thrilling work at Dunkirk and in the south of England, provided few day raids, for Hull was out of range of dive bombers or fighter escourts. But there was constant mine-laying, with many small and inept raids inland.

From the AA defence point of view it was an interesting time. More and more of their customers were night birds, and as the black-out doping of night-flyers was not universal the Searchlights had a busy and productive time. The number of guns then available, and the methods of using them by night, prevented the heavy AA from being a very successful weapon. The R.A.F. fighter was the best killer, and on every suitable night all possible help which AA units could give was concentrated on assisting the night-fighters, with eminently satisfactory results. Illuminations and interceptions were frequent, and the percentage of German machines shot down was satisfactorily high. The Searchlights also enabled several enemy 'planes to be shot down by the heavy AA guns; and in addition Searchlight Batteries, especially those in the Spurn and Grimsby area, were of constant value for their speed and accuracy in recognising friend or foe in the sky by day or night, by sight or sound, and reporting them. Any AA or R.A.F. Commander will tell you the value of a report which establishes the identity of approaching aircraft.

Searchlight sites were often bombed during this period, but nothing suffered much except crockery, rations and the cook's temper. One attack scored a direct hit on a searchlight in action, the bulk of which was later recognised with difficulty some 80 yards away. No. 4 and No. 5 were in the emplacement and were buried, but miraculously were alive when dug out. The Detachment were shaken up; but they drew a new searchlight next morning and, with the exception of No. 5 who was in hospital, were engaging raiders again that night. On another site, a bomb wrecked the cookhouse but made an excellent duck pond for the Detachment livestock.

By September the combined action of R.A.F. Fighters and A.A, Units had obviously made this area so dangerous that raiders usually swung well clear to the north or south of the Humber as soon as they had made their landfall. Throughout the autumn this state of affairs continued, German attacks being light apart from mine-laying, and long hours of cold nights were spent trying to manoeuvre evasive Germans into areas where guns or fighters could have at them. On the ground it was a busy time. A new Searchlight policy entailed endless digging, moving huts and training. Heavy AA and light AA were all but overwhelmed by a huge intake of civilians whom they converted into soldiers without relaxing their operational work. A new method of Fire Control was studied, introduced and developed, and Humber heavy AA put much original work into its development. Much was done to assist the Navy in preventing and locating mine-layers. The problem of the blacked-out bomber was constantly with them, for the many raids which have been lightly passed over were each of them a very real anxiety. And so ended 1940, in ice and snow, like its predecessor - and the Humber can be cold. Humber AA defences had acted largely as handmaid to the R.A.F. and to the Navy, and as nursemaid in its own establishment. Though the enemy 'planes brought down by the guns were still in single figures, they had helped in many hunts where the actual kill was entered in another game book.

Humber suffers as a "stand" because a gun loses so many of his birds in the water; but it was a good and exciting time which lasted till losses such as the above, with many others which could not be seen and substantiated, drove the Hun away to do his mine-laying in less expensive areas. Heavy AA shared in the bag but the light AA had most of the fun at this time. One of their Sergeants gave an excellent broadcast on it.

February, March and April were packed with raids, mine-laying raids, raids on Hull and raids on other parts of the area. On March 22nd a daylight raider, who had lost his way, came out of low clouds over a well-defended area inland. A hot reception drove him back into the clouds unhurt. His next descent from the clouds found him in the very centre of the Humber area with Heaven knows how many fingers itching on their triggers. Light machine-gun fire instantly wrecked both engines and killed the observer. The pilot just had time to release his bombs before he hit a tree. Somehow he got out alive. Everyone claimed this 'plane, but an extremely tough Light AA Subaltern got there first and abolished the claim of the Balloon Barrage. It was eventually allotted to his Troop, though the work may well have been shared by a Lewis Gunner of the Searchlights, who apologised to his Colonel for shooting in front of the target. All through these months R.A.F. fighters were co-operating as before, but these low flyers were more the guns' meat than theirs. There is a satisfactory list of enemy 'planes engaged by the R.A.F. with and without AA co-operation from January to April.

Blitz attacks had been an anxiety for some time. A fire control team, sent out from Humber to assist in training other gun zones, had brought back first-hand information from Coventry. Sheffield, a sister gun-zone, handed on the lessons learnt there. Continual thought and work had been given to the problem, and May brought full trial to Humber AA Defences. Each night from the 2nd to the 6th saw some activity, and on May 7th and 8th there were really serious attacks lasting between four and five hours. On each night lire bombs fell first and then H.E. was dropped into the fire area.

The first night was a broadcast affair, doing much damage and causing fires here, there and everywhere throughout Hull. The second attack appeared to be far better carried out; either the fires still burning helped the Germans, or better squadrons were used, or possibly ginger had been distributed for the rather slipshod bombing of the night before. Incendiaries started fires near the centre of the town, and bombing worked steadily eastward parallel with the river, firing stack after stack of timber. High explosives followed accurately in the path of the incendiaries and soon there appeared to be five miles of flame, punctuated by the flashes of bombs, and more encouragingly by those of guns and shells. Early on the first night communications were badly deranged; but steps taken beforehand enabled an efficient tactical and technical control of guns and searchlights to be maintained throughout both nights.

From the defence point of view results were disappointing on the first night. Nothing had quite worked; although there were many reports of enemy casualties, few could be substantiated; but in any case all were too busy putting things right to worry overmuch about claiming casualties. The second night was one of clear cold moonlight, with a red glow and a black pall of smoke over Hull. Highflying Huns left vapour trails, which could be seen with the naked eye. If the Hun had improved his technique, so had we; and with one or two minor hitches our carefully thought-out plans worked. Soon after the attack began, wireless messages were coming through from pilot after pilot of Huns engaged and falling, each checked up a few seconds later by searchlight reports of machines falling in flames. Nor were the guns idle : they shot down only one less than the R.A.F. that night. No third attack came, despite the fires that burnt. Had it come, all was ready to raise the scale of Hun casualties once more. Hull had been hammered but had hit back.

There was much gallantry abroad those two nights, first and foremost among A.R.P. and A.F.S. personnel, who kept damage, and casualties down and courage up by their untiring and undismayed work in these as in all other raids. When the first attack began those at "C" heavy AA site not serving the guns were celebrating a visit of the Brigade Concert Party, followed by a dance. It was a pre-war "militia" site, better furnished with huts than the war-time model. As the guns opened, the Battery Commander walked towards the Canteen to warn civilian guests that a raid was on. A sentry suddenly dashed past him shouting a warning. Hardly were the words out of his mouth before there was an almighty crash and half the camp went up.

The first thing the Battery Commander heard as he picked himself up was the National Anthem being sung in the remains of the wrecked canteen to end the concert, and the voice of an N.C.O. turning out and organising the fire piquet. The camp caught fire from end to end, and the blaze was far more than local appliances could cope with. Armed with axes, crowbars and bare hands, Officers, Warrant Officers, N.C.Os. and all who could be spared from the guns, including two prisoners from the Guard Room, broke into collapsed and blazing huts, dragged out stunned men who had been trapped there and rendered first aid. Back came the Hun, showering incendiaries, but the workers were too busy to notice them at the time. Four men were killed and a dozen injured; but without the superhuman efforts which seem to have come naturally to everybody at the time, some 50 or 60 would have died in the burning camp. Throughout, the guns of "C" Station continued their engagement of the enemy. And the A.T.S. kept making tea. One is glad to record that on the next night this Station scored a direct hit on an enemy 'plane which exploded and came down in fragments.

Down in the Docks a Light AA Detachment kept their gun in action, firing whenever the billowing smoke gave them a chance. In the intervals they saved their own M.T. and much else from fire and dealt with incendiaries as these arrived. Soon a very near miss severely wounded both M.T. drivers and caused several minor casualties. The Subaltern in command handed the gun over to the Sergeant and drove them through a rain of H.E. and incendiaries, past or through bomb-holes, negotiating fallen tram and telephone poles and cables, past shattered and blazing buildings. He got his men to hospital, had his own wound dressed, returned to his site and resumed command.

The good barge Clem, which with her sister ship the Humph, mounts searchlight and Lewis gun and leads an exciting life in the Humber, shot down a raider which came screaming out of the artillery concentration into the fancied security of the river.

There are many more tales of these two nights - tales of medical orderlies and drivers, tales of signallers mending cables under fire, tales of officers, cooks and clerks tripping and sweating in the cold night to carry ammunition or make recalcitrant guns "run out" to the firing position. There are tales of gallantry but also of clear heads used with determination.

Small raids continued during May, but were dealt with by the guns and did little damage. June, July and August saw continuous enemy activity in the area and an increasing percentage of enemy machines shot down, chiefly by heavy AA, but with Bofors and Lewis guns scoring when the chance came to them. Late June and July brought a series of well-executed enemy raids by 35 to 50 'planes each time, which caused considerable damage until an answer was found to the method of attack used. During one of these raids heavy AA fire shook up a raider at 10,000 feet; he lost height rapidly and was picked up by a searchlight south of the river. The enemy dived on the searchlight, dropping incendiaries and high explosives, one of which pitched 50 yards from the site and knocked the Subaltern and Lewis Gunner off their feet. The searchlight held the 'plane, which circled as if to attack again; but the Subaltern picked himself up, ran to the gun, and his bullets finished the engagement, for the 'plane dived and crashed. After August, Germany's other interests gave Humber its quietest time since the beginning of 1940, but the few Huns who came within range suffered a high percentage of casualties. The bag for 1941 was several times greater than for 1940.

The story ends with a footnote in the first person. "We have done our share of killing, in addition to 'driving' for the R.A.F.. Much of our work is unknown and done in the dark, trying to help Bomber or Fighter in case of need. Signallers work endlessly so that no point in the game be lost; despatch riders face night, snow, fog and slippery roads so that essential orders of the day reach every site. What I write may seem poor comfort to the people of much-blitzed Hull, yet our close co-operation and good fellowship with the civilian population is of the best. They realise our difficulties and our efforts, and their tough, cheerful, Yorkshire spirit does the rest. We cannot say we have kept the enemy away; no air or ground defence yet invented can say that, but there are many raiders which have turned away and many bombs which have fallen harshly in fields or water. We have done our best to use the men, the resources and the brains available, we have tried never to stand still but to progress, we have shared the dangers and we have hit back. And we are still of the same mind and of the same determination."

These are the men, duplicated all over the British Isles, who made sure that, though the Bomber may "always get through," he does not always get home.

- C H A P T E R 1 4 -
THE GREAT LONDON BARRAGE

THE BATTLE of Britain was still in full swing when the first night attack was made on London on September 6th/7th, 1940. The daylight battles had begun to go against the Germans, though they were still continuing them.

London at this time was not adequately defended. All over England there was still a shortage of anti-aircraft guns, and as we might be attacked anywhere, it was essential to give cover to all our large cities. In the Thames Estuary a considerable concentration of anti-aircraft guns had been built up, because many of the German daylight attacks were made via the Thames Estuary. But now it was essential that the gun defence of London should be rapidly improved. Within 24 hours of the first night attack reinforcements from all over the country were on their way to London, and within 48 hours the guns in London had been doubled.

The initial attacks on London were made on the East End docks and caused very great havoc. It appeared as if the enemy thought that by concentrating on the East End, where there was a large and crowded population, he would cause such panic as to endanger the Government's position, if not to force them to make peace. Thanks to the stubbornness, first of the people in the East End, and later of all Londoners, this indiscriminate bombing of the civilian population did not result in any serious loss of morale. At the same time, the very courage of the Londoner constituted an obligation to defend him.

AA guns take a little time to be effective after they have moved into new positions. Telephone lines have to be laid, gun positions levelled and the warning system coordinated; it was, therefore, disappointing that, though the reinforcements in guns by the second night of the battle were very considerable, there did not appear to he much more AA fire.

Before the war a very complicated system of barrages, depending primarily on sound locators for their information, had been organised. It was known as the "Fixed Azimuth" system.

Special regiments had been trained in its use, and during the early stages of the war it had been improved very greatly. But, depending as it did on sound for its information, it was both inaccurate and cumbersome, and it could only produce a small volume of fire for the large number of guns.

During the nights of September 8th and 9th, Command and Divisional staffs visited gun sites and consulted together in Gun Operations Rooms in order to try and produce a more effective answer to the German night raids. But, though variations of all sorts were put into effect on the night of the 9th with a view to

A firefighter in London during the battle of Britain

producing greater accuracy, everyone on the Command and Divisional staffs was most dissatisfied with the results. Early on the morning of the 10th, a conference was held at Command headquarters with the determination that, whatever had gone before, on that Wednesday night the enemy should be met with a barrage the like of which had never been seen or heard before. Great difficulties were still encountered. Radiolocation, though it had been progressing marvellously, was still in its infancy, and very few gun positions were equipped even with the radio warning sets. Even sound locators, which were in use with the "Fixed Azimuth" system, were really only capable of giving the height at which the enemy was travelling perhaps ten miles away from the Capital; on the gun site itself there was no method of finding out whether the height had changed.

After a very earnest consultation with scientists and experts of all sorts a meeting was called in London for 12.30 that day. The Gun Position Officers (i.e., the officers in charge of firing the guns) from every site in London were directed to attend, in addition to the Battery, Brigade and Divisional Commanders. It was made a point of honour with these G.P.Os. - many of them young officers who a few months before had been civilians - that, however handicapped they might be by shortage of equipment, they should put up such a barrage that night as, if it did nothing else, would hearten the civilian population. All the schemes that the scientists could devise were explained to them; and as a final bit of advice they were told that, where all else failed, they would get a height sent to them from the Gun Operations Room and they must use their ears to estimate where the enemy was, and then barrage in front of them at that height.

The result was remarkable. Punctually to time the German bombers arrived - and were met by a roar of guns which must have astonished them as much as it heartened the Londoners. The enemy had been flying at 1,200 feet; as soon as the barrage opened they climbed to 22,000 feet. Many turned back and at least nine 'planes were shot down by AA fire. Guns were in action all night; and at dawn, as the ammunition lorries moved into the sites to replenish the unprecedented number of rounds which had been fired, the gunners were washing out the hot bores of their guns.

The Regional Commissioner had been warned that there would be a great deal of heavy fire in London that night, so that he could get the wardens in charge of the shelters to explain it. There was, however, no need for this precaution. Everywhere in London people said, "Thank God we are fighting back." Though the number of enemy aircraft destroyed that night was not large in proportion to the prodigious number of rounds fired, the morale of London jumped 100 per cent. The next morning every newspaper came out with emblazoned headlines on London's barrage.

On that barrage, so crudely begun, has been built up the most effective defence that all our scientific brains could produce. It has, moreover, become a pattern for the defence not only of the cities of Great Britain, but our fortresses abroad and the cities of other mighty adherents to the United Nations.

The best tribute to the barrage from Londoners is the remark heard on every side the next day, "I never slept so peacefully in my life as when I heard those guns booming!"

The Command was so short of men during the winter of 1940-41 that to a certain extent London had to be reinforced with recruits strange to gunnery and unfamiliar with fire discipline. Take the specimen case of a battery stationed at Cleethorpes, where for many weeks it had kept watch over the Humber without being called upon to fire a round. It was ordered to London. Twenty-five hours later the battery was on its new site - a site almost completely unprepared. Ground, clogged with bricks, mortar and stone, had to be levelled. Guns had to be laid down, instruments connected up, and supplies of ammunition arranged. A 3-ton R.A.S.C. lorry was pressed into use as a men's canteen and another as a sergeants' mess. By 7.30 p.m. all essential work had been done and the guns were ready.

At 8.15 p.m. the alarm was given. The battery opened with a barrage which had to be worked out on the spot, as ready communication with a central control was not available. At 6 a.m. the order "Stand Easy!" was given, to the relief of four gun teams of dead-beat men. But it was only "Stand Easy!" as far as action was concerned. There was work to be done in boiling out, servicing and polishing the guns. It was 9.30 a.m. before the men went to sleep, in tents, with the bare ground as their bed. Half an hour later came the first of many daylight alarms; and each time, so near the bare existence-line was that mobile battery, the same men had to take posts. For eight days the procedure was the same. Alarms by day, continuous barraging by night, and so little sleep that at times the layers were almost unconscious as they tried to keep their eyes focused on the dials.

On the ninth day relief came, in the shape of troops who had done no more than the basic military training that precedes every AA man's introduction to gunnery. Only two hours were available in which to instruct them in their duties. The question was how they would react when the enemy was engaged. To be on a gun in action for the first time can be unnerving. Older hands stood near them as they applied bearing and elevation for their first shots in the night battle of London. But after three rounds had been fired the older hands were ordered to fall out.

A battery manning 4.5-inch guns on the Isle of Dogs caught the brunt of the big attack on the London Docks on September 7th. Many of the gunners had been in uniform only a few weeks. In fact, when the first warning came through from Gun Operations Room, Captain Fletcher, the site commander, was inspecting a fresh intake of men who had never before been on a gun position. Their training was to be expedited by events. For three days and nights the action raged. Right at the beginning a heavy bomb landed on the road leading to their guns, ruling out any chance of transport getting through with supplies. Their greatest worry was ammunition replenishment, but the R.A.S.C. lorries arrived regularly and the gunners carried every round a hundred yards over the bomb-torn ground to their gun-pits.

Captain W. J. S. Fletcher was given the immediate award of the M.C. for his courage, leadership and devotion to duty. In the short lulls between actions he went out searching the site and the devastated neighbourhood for unexploded bombs which threatened both men and equipment. Frequently he led parties of gunners to deal with explosive incendiary bombs. There was not a hope of putting out the fires which ringed and lit up the site, but he kept many of them under control.

In those days conditions on gun sites, though better than at the beginning of the war, were still not very good. The majority were deep in mud, and the gunners lived in crude dug-outs immediately beside the gun-pits. Blast from the guns soon told on these quarters. Many of them collapsed, and nearly all of them soon became so badly warped from bomb and gun blast that it was useless attempting to pump out the rain-water.

At one point in the Battle of London the enemy concentrated on gun sites. Although bombing was severe and several sites received either direct or nearby hits, the total casualties were very slight and there was relatively small damage to equipment. Not one battery was put out of action. Seventy-three H.Es. fell within a quarter of a mile of one site; on another site three heavy bombs exploded over the guns. Barrack huts and stores were destroyed, and in some eases communications were interrupted. On a site in the South-east a bomb landed outside the guard-room, shattering a complete row of huts. Immediately afterwards a Molotov Breadbasket unloaded itself over the camp. Twenty tires flared up; but the lire piquet, aided by the A.F.S., put them out before much harm had been done.

A week after the London barrages first flowered came the peak of the daylight attacks. Sunday, September 15th was one of our lighter pilots' great days. The enemy attacked with more than 500 'planes, at that time the largest force ever launched in a single day's offensive, and lost at least 185 of them. Here is the anti-aircraft side of the picture.

In the morning attack the guns could play little part because of the presence of friendly fighters, though, of course, they did their usual job in breaking up formations. Their opportunity came in the afternoon. At about 2.30 p.m. the first of two great waves of enemy 'planes, each more than 150 strong, crossed the coast between Dover and Dungeness, and thrust towards the Thames Estuary. Less than a hundred of them managed to elude the fighter net and reach the southeastern outskirts of London. Eight minutes after crossing the coast it was apparent that they were headed straight for the Chatham guns. There was not long to wait. Distant thuds came in quick succession as the West Mailing guns engaged them. A curtain of white puffs, remote and unreal, shrouded the toy-like -peeks. One of them fell away trailing black smoke. Now they could be identified through binoculars, about 40 Dornier 215s in close arrowhead formation with their fighters, flying at 18,000 feet and 250 m.p.h.

The Staff officers who provided the material for this story were watching from one of the old forts of Chatham, built to repel an earlier invasion which never came.

The bombers came steadily on. The range shortened. From the sunlit town there was neither noise nor movement.

Then the outer gun stations went into action. The black bursts of the first salvoes sprang up among the leading bombers. The foremost Dornier swerved and dived away, a long plume of smoke trailing from its cockpit. From the engines of the second came thin wisps of white smoke that grew to a cloud. The formation turned away from the wall of bursts towards the Medway, climbing steadily and spreading widely like the fingers of an outstretched hand. One of them exploded with a direct hit, and a string of flaming fragments fell towards the river. More and more gun stations took up the action: there was an infernal crescendo of sound. For half a minute - how disproportionately short these significant battles are - the Dorniers pressed on in formation.

Then, over Dartford, the close wedge was broken, and as the bombers scattered to avoid the bursting shells.

Hurricanes and Spitfires, diving out of the sun, did execution.

Meanwhile to the south-west of Chatham a second wave of Heinkels was similarly faltering under intense gun-fire. Long before the Medway was reached its ranks had degenerated into a straggling line, widely dispersed.

For some minutes the cloudy sky above the Isle of Grain was the setting for high drama.

The routed Dorniers of the first wave were staggering about in dogfights, the sky a wild medley of twisting aircraft. The white discs of parachutes hung in the air.

Over Chatham the guns still held the stage and the Heinkels of the second wave rocked and jinked as they tried to run the gauntlet of the barking inner guns and the cruisers in the river.

The leading Heinkel, caught in a salvo of 3.7-inch shells with its bomb-load still in the racks, blew to pieces at 19,000 feet.

Almost at the same instant another Heinkel, hit in the cockpit and engines, fell flaming down towards Dartford Park. Thirty seconds later, over the Isle of Sheppey, the guns shot away the tail of a third machine which dived 5,000 feet into the sea and disappeared entirely. The guns had shot down three raiders in less than three minutes.

Not far away the Bofors gunners engaged a Dornier flying fast and low towards the sea. Repeated hits were scored; the target danced antics in the air; both engines caught fire, and he turned over and fell towards the sea. The air at this time was full of the crumps of bursting salvoes, the whine of falling shell splinters, the uproar of engines. And as the London batteries engaged, the din was multiplied.

A third wave of enemy approached, mainly Dorniers, at slightly over 16,000 feet. This was the last mass-formation attack of the day. It was not a mass formation for long. It was quickly scattered by the guns, and while out of range of the majority of batteries, the enemy turned away westwards to meet the Nemesis of further fighter squadrons.

In the mopping-up actions, when the returning enemy came within range at all, two more Dorniers and a Messerschmitt 109 fell to the heavy guns and two Dorniers to the light AA batteries. It is not possible to detail all the incidents of that crowded half-hour which, of course, seemed like hours of battle to the people who took part. A fugitive Dornier appeared out of the clouds over a Bofors position to be shot down in flames only 500 yards from the gun-pit. A Messerschmitt, its tail shot away at 15,000 feet, whined down to shatter itself in a rural churchyard. Another Dornier, already hit in the port engine, blundered over Chatham at 5,000 feet. As the 4.5-inch bursts sprang up beside it, pieces of wing and fuselage broke away from it. Four occupants baled out and were captured by cheering civilians who raced across the fields while the pilotless bomber, skimming the roof-tops, buried itself in a cottage garden.

Shortly before five o'clock the gunners of a cargo vessel steaming down the river hit a Heinkel with their twelve-pounder at 200 yards' range, and saw it crash into the mudflats on the Essex side of the river.

During these late engagements cloud almost completely covered the sky and visibility grew gradually worse. It was under these conditions that the last action of the day took place. At 5.15 p.m. a single Dornier 215 dived from low cloud, cracking away with its machine gun at the streets of an estuary town. At 3,000 feet a Bofors opened up and brought it down flaming - a red exclamation mark to close the story of a memorable day.

CHAPTER 15

PORTSMOUTH FIGHTS BACK

I HAVE traced the progress of the German air offensive through its successive stages up to the culminating day. Broadly speaking, whatever type of objective the enemy chose (he switched from one type to another at quite short intervals) he was baffled by a defence in which the gunners played their full part. After his defeat on September 15th it is possible, perhaps, to detect yet another change in objectives. Instead of attacking categories of things, such as ships, docks or airfields, the enemy tended to attack places, or in the phrase which the Russians have made famous, "inhabited localities," and to attack them by night instead of by day. These concentrated blitzes led to the coining of a new verb, to coventrate, from the spectacular night blitz on Coventry. All such attacks are very similar in character. When one has been described, all have been described. We hope, therefore, that nobody's feelings will be hurt if we select as a specimen one of the so far lesser known of these attacks, and tell the story of Portsmouth.

The late winter and early spring of 1940-41 had been fairly quiet. After a big raid on Southampton on December 1st, there was a tailing-off in enemy activity. By day the *Luftwaffe* concentrated on reconnaissance and attacks on shipping. By night his efforts were sporadic. This quiet spell continued throughout January and February, and it was not until the night of March 8th that big-scale air attack flared up.

This attack was directed against Portsmouth, and the enemy's objective was the destruction of certain battleships as they lay in port. Some days before the attack a single scouting 'plane had come over regularly to keep an eye on the battleships. Then, at 7 p.m. on March 8th, the bombers came. Passing Portsmouth to the east, they flew north to Portsdown Hill, where, using the white gash of a quarry as their turning point, they swooped south to the attack. Six separate raids were made before the enemy gave up.

The next night they returned in greater force. Flying in formations of three or four 'planes, they came half an hour later and kept up the attack for four hours. Naval as well as Ack-Ack guns were in action, and their fire was so fierce - the Solent heavy guns alone put up 1,421 rounds - that the bombers rave up diving and had to content themselves with high-level bombing.

They attacked again the next night, for six hours, and received such a pounding from the Solent guns that, although they returned on the following night, the edge had been taken from their determination. Four enemy 'planes were shot down by the guns. The raiders came in from Dieppe at heights varying from 9,000 to 22,000 feet. The night was clear, and the larger bombers could easily be seen silhouetted in the brilliant moonlight. Searchlights had previously been grouped round Portsmouth in pairs in an attempt to put bomb-aimers off their marks by dazzling them. But, although there were four short illuminations, the smoke which was soon rising from many fires hampered this tactic. From 8.47 p.m. fighters were operating over the gun-defended area from 14,000 feet upwards and consequently the guns were not shooting at targets over 12,000 feet. After an hour, however, the guns were again given permission to engage at any height. A feature of the raid was the use of a new type of incendiary bomb which burst 20 or 30 feet above the ground and threw out a shower of blazing magnesium.

Despite the ferocity of the attack - "our concrete command post was rocking like a ship at sea," said one Gun Position Officer - the Gunners had so far gone unscathed. Then, just before the engagement ended, two heavy bombs fell on an AA site. One of the bombs landed in the height-finder emplacement and shattered the command post. An officer, a sergeant and nine other ranks were killed. The second bomb fell just outside one of the gun-pits, spraying the crew with splinters and wrecking the hut. Although all the instruments and one of the guns were out of action, and men were trying desperately to save their coMr.ades in the wrecked command post, the Battery continued to engage the enemy with two guns. Captain K. Bermingham and Second-Lieutenant D. Reeds took charge of a gun each - there were not enough men left to man the third - and maintained a steady fire with gun control.

Second-Lieutenant V. Rose was wounded by a bomb splinter which struck the back of his tin hat; but he continued to rescue men from the wrecked post until he collapsed. He was to lie paralysed in hospital for four months.

When the raiders came again the following night, Major R. N. Guest, Officer Commanding, and Captain Bermingham directed operations not from a command post, which obviously could not be built in time, but from a trestle table set up in the middle of the Gun Park. There, by the light of a hurricane lamp, they sat before a graphic range table measuring out their fuses with a piece of string. A steady flow of hostile 'planes came in from the south and crossed the Solent, most of them continuing northwards to the Midlands. Again there was a clear sky and bright moonlight. H.Es. and incendiaries were dropped over a wide area by 'planes flying between 6,500 and 20,000 feet. At 10 p.m. several antipersonnel bombs fell on one of the gun sites. Most of them fell harmlessly about the camp, but one landed inside a gun emplacement, damaging the gun and killing nine other ranks who were in action at the time. Two officers and three other ranks were wounded. On that night the Solent guns fired a record number of shells - 3,653.

During the rest of March there was no big-scale activity over the Solent, although the guns were kept busy firing on 'birds of passage' bound for the Midlands and the North.

It was on the night of April 17th that the enemy again struck at Portsmouth. Raiders droned over almost without interruption from 9.12 p.m. until 4.25 a.m. Great numbers of bombs were dropped, but the attack misfired badly. Most of the high explosive bombs and incendiaries, with which they sought to wipe out the naval dockyards and the city around them, fell on flat, open fields where they did no harm.

One of the first showers of incendiaries released fell in a half-circle round a gun site. The glare of the blazing incendiaries drew the bombers like moths to a candle flame, and one after another came over to release its load. More than thirty heavy bombs fell on the fields within a quarter of a mile radius of the gun site, but it was not until later in the action that the site was hit. Two fell among the huts, smashing them to matchwood, and a third landed between the command post and the No. 2 gun, which it put out of action, killing some members of the crew. The predictor, in an emplacement next to the Command Post, was also put out of action. A fourth bomb blew in the back of the cabin as the crew sat at the controls. They escaped with a bad shaking.

The Battery continued to engage the enemy 'planes, which were now swooping very low over the position. Some came as low as 600 feet, and one big four-engined bomber was fired on by the guard with their rifles. Two of the remaining three guns went out of action, leaving only the Number 4 gun, christened "Annie" by the crew, still firing. Under its Number One, Bombardier Robert

Wrecked German aircraft (Me 109E, He 111 and Ju 88A) in Britain, 1940.

Hart, it fired on gun control at parachute flares, hitting three out of six. H.Es. and incendiaries were still being rained on the position, and at last orders were given to evacuate the site.

Before leaving their gun Bombardier Hart and his men made a gesture. They went through the formal drill of going to a standby bearing and marched out of the gun-pit as if they had just finished an hour's silent practice. They then joined the fire-fighting squad.

Six men of the Battery were killed and a number wounded. That the casualties were not far larger was due to the good luck that, though hundreds of incendiaries were dropped, not one fell on the splintered woodwork of the wrecked huts. If they had fallen there they would have lighted a beacon, which would have drawn every bomber in the area. During the night the Solent guns claimed two Category I hits (certainly destroyed) and two Category II (probably destroyed). One Junkers 88 crashed with its full bomb-load and blew up. The number of rounds fired by the Solent guns was the highest since the big raid on March 11th - 2,771 rounds of 3.7 and 4.5 ammunition.

CHAPTER 16

THE SUPPORT SERVICES OF FIGHTER COMMAND

EVERY PILOT that flew his fighter aircraft into battle, and every aircraft that flew in the skies against this formidable enemy was supported by thousands of civilian and military personnel in the support teams. Without them, these fighter aircraft and their pilots would never have left the ground on operational duties. For every Spitfire or Hurricane to become airborne and fly of into battle, nearly two hundred people would have been responsible for keeping it in the air and getting it safely back to its base. These support teams were the unsung heroes of the Battle of Britain. They worked behind the scenes, many of them throughout the nights to keep Britain's defence system working.

Some of these support teams are:

- The designers and engineers at Supermarine, Hawker and Rolls Royce
- The radio designers and technicians who strove to improve communications
- The fitters and engineers of the R.A.F. ground staff
- The refuellers of the R.A.F. ground staff
- The armourers of the R.A.F. ground staff
- The CRT operators at the radar stations
- The servicemen of the Observer Corps
- The radio operators and plotters in the filter rooms
- The personnel of the Anti-Aircraft Regiments
- The R.A.F. Intelligence
- The Air Transport Auxiliary
- The doctors, nurses and ambulance drivers
- Civilian gas, electricity and water technicians
- The many civilians who helped crash-landed pilots get back to their bases

All these people in some way or another assisted to keep the aircraft flying and in the air. Women too, were to play their part, often preferred as radar operators and plotters because they appeared to be far more sharp and accurate than their male counterparts. Women also drove cars, trucks and even flew aircraft in a ferrying capacity, but they were never allowed to fly on combat operations.

Listed below, are some of the factors that were to play a very important part in Fighter Command during the Battle of Britain.

RADAR

Air Chief Marshal Hugh Dowding, gaining on his personal experience in the First World War when he was a squadron commander, he could see some of the disadvantages when it came to defence. He spoke of the times when you did not know when the enemy would attack until they were over your lines and within visual sighting distance... and your aircraft were still on the ground!!

"If only we knew when they were coming... we could be up in the air and waiting for them" he said. He mentioned that they did have forward observation posts, but communications left much to be desired and many messages that should have alerted us of the enemy approaching never got through to us.

It was back in 1934 that the Army acoustics section had devised two huge dishes some 200 feet long and 25 feet high and placed them on the high ground of Romney Marsh in Kent facing out towards the channel. Each of these dishes had microphones fitted along the entire length and were supposed to pick up sound waves of approaching aircraft. The experiment proved that such a venture was not at all practical as it could hardly pick up the sound of approaching test aircraft flying at 7,000 feet and at only 65-70 miles per hour. Not only that, it did pick up sounds of nearby motor cars, boats offshore and the hundreds of sea birds that frequent the cliffs along the coastline.

That same year, at the Air Ministry, there was a Mr. H. Wimperis a scientific research director and a Mr. A.P. Rowe who was on Mr. Wimperis's staff. Mr. Rowe, on studying the records at the Air Ministry were astounded to find that there were less than fifty documents out of thousands that related to the subject of air defence. Because of the importance of defence, Mr. Wimperis suggested to the Air Ministry that a committee be formed. This was approved and the committee under the chairmanship of a well known physicist, Mr. Henry Tizzard with both Rowe and Wimperis on the committee.

Wimperis considered many alternatives, from perfecting the sound locaters that were tried earlier in 1934, to something along the lines of a "Death Ray" often mentioned in science fiction books. On these matters Wimperis consulted a Robert Watson-Watt who had worked for a number of years on high frequency radio signals. Watson-Watt did not completely discount the theory of the "Death Ray", but had previously come up with the idea in tests that short wave radio signals that were transmitted had been interfered with by aeroplanes, where the signal was bounced off the aircraft and reflected the signal back. Watson-Watt suggested that this theory could be worked on with the possibility that the radio signal being bounced back could be picked up by a receiver and the impulses then displayed on a cathode ray tube. This way, because of the length of time that it took a signal to be returned and picked up by the receiver, it would be possible to determine the distance from signal source to aircraft.

The theory seemed possible, and the committee looked upon the suggestion with great enthusiasm. But, as Wimperis pointed out to Watson-Watt and Hugh Dowding who was then Air member for Research and Development, holding the rank then of Air Vice Marshal, that all this was simply just theory as no such instrument had yet been designed or constructed. Dowding was full of enthusiasm, and even more so later when Watson-Watt said that he could get hold of a BBC short wave transmitter of just ten kilowatts at Daventry. By setting up a receiver and a cathode ray tube twenty miles distant, it was hoped that the theory would work by using a light bomber as the enemy aircraft.

On February 26th 1935, a full test was arranged. A Heyford light bomber flew along a pre-determined line and the scientists stood holding their breath as they had no idea if the theory would work. Then suddenly a green line appeared on the screen, it moved from right to left for a while then as the aircraft turned and came towards them the line got sightly bigger and bigger. They were elated. Without looking for a visual sighting of the aircraft, they watched the cathode ray tube oscillograph, that looked something like a small television set. They could track the Heyford bomber without even looking up into the skies.

This was the beginning of radar, the first time that such a test had been conducted and it gave Watson-Watt and his team something to build on. Radio waves sent out by the transmitter were reflected back from the bomber and were displayed on the CRT screen. The small green line indicated that the aircraft was some distance away, but as the aircraft got closer the line got bigger. The results were very promising and when word got back to the Department of Research and Development, Dowding was elated with the results saying "If we can produce such apparatus it would become the 'eyes' of our defence system and the greatest innovation we could dream of."

Over the next three years, the team of Wimperis, Watson-Watt and Rowe concentrated on radio direction finding. There were a few disappointments, and there were successes in further tests, but slowly it was all coming together. Once it was discovered that they could determine the height and direction of detected aircraft, further work was carried out in getting this information to the various departments so that the R.A.F. could dispatch aircraft quickly and meet the intruders before they reached the British coast. Radar, as it became known, although its correct name was Radio Direction Finding (RDF) had been born.

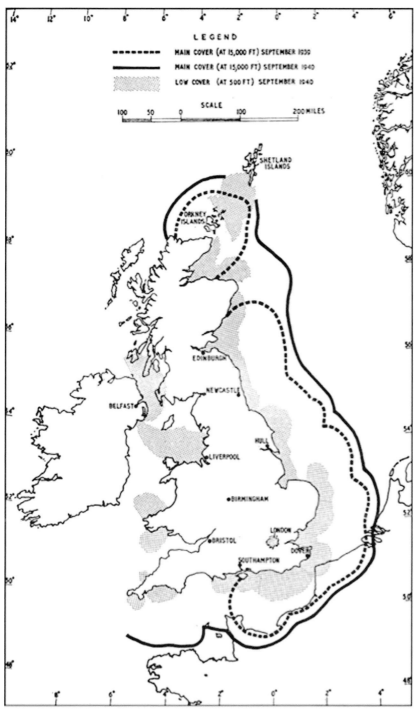

Map showing British radar range between Sep 1939 and Sep 1940.

THE OBSERVER CORPS

'Early stone age' was Churchill's description in 1939 of the aircraft-warning system over land. He was then visiting Bawdsey to see the progress of radar. The great towers on the coast could look far out to sea, but behind them over the countryside and towns they were almost blind.

Special constables who were members of the Observer Corps spent many hours of their spare time watching from hill-tops and plotting in stuffy rooms. They would doubtless have been incensed at Churchill's remark, but, Stone Age or not, their work was vital. Where radar ended at the coast the whole weight of responsibility for accurate records of aircraft movements lay with the Observer Corps and its telephone network.

In the early days of the 'Corps', its compliment was generally made up of special constables and constables who voluntarily gave up their spare time and went 'aeroplane watching'. But as it was realised that all responsibility was passed on to them after enemy aircraft had crossed the coast, more and more people were drafted into the 'Corps' and it became a military establishment controlled by Fighter Command.

In total, the Observer Corps boasted a strength of over 32,000 men and between then manned in excess of 1,400 command posts scattered all around the coastal areas of Britain, although the bulk of them were posted to the southern and south-eastern coast around Hampshire, Sussex, Kent and Essex.

Their main duties were to observe, locate and estimate enemy aircraft strength, height and direction. But other important duties were to report the location of crashed aircraft of both the R.A.F. and the *Luftwaffe*. They also had to watch out for pilots that had parachuted to safety and accurately observe their location, especially if they happen to be out over the sea. This speeded up the process of the R.A.F. Air-Sea Rescue or Coastal Command reaching pilots before they either suffered from water immersion or before they drowned. This was especially the case should the pilot have sustained any serious injury.

The men of the Observer Corps, which was given the prefix "Royal" in 1941 made a valuable contribution to the Battle of Britain, for without them Fighter Command would have been 'blind' once enemy aircraft formations had crossed the coast.

One of the problems of the Radar Stations, was that their beams were directed out to sea and away from the coast. This was fine, as radar could pick up and track hostile aircraft as soon as they were leaving the French coast and making their way across the Channel. But, as soon as they were over the English coast, the enemy was no longer in the hands of radar. Of course, radar could not detect how many aircraft there were, nor could they supply any information as to type and exact height. This task was left to a band of men, looking skywards and visually making a 'sighting' and reporting their findings to a central command post. This band of highly trained and skilled men were to be known as The Observer Corps.

The Corps was by no means new. In fact their history would go back to the beginning of First World War, where at that time it was the Royal Naval Air Service that was responsible for Britain's home defence. It was the duty of the local police to act as observers and report to the Admiralty any sightings of enemy aircraft. Of course, they were by no means skilled operators at this and quite often many unidentified aircraft were reported, and on many an occasion, being as the policeman had to report by telephone which we must remember were not in every home as they are today, so by the time he had found a telephone and made his report the aircraft could have travelled many miles and even changed its course. By the middle of the war, the Admiralty had handed over to the Army, and the Royal Flying Corps was in operation, the police had been relinquished of their observer duties and it was handed over to civilians who were spaced at regular intervals around what was interpreted as 'important and vulnerable' targets. With the Army now in control, all sightings had to be reported to the War Office. It was not until 1921 that these civilians were given the title of Observer Corps, a title that was to stay with them when Hugh Dowding took over Fighter Command in 1936.

Dowding saw the importance of the Observer Corps and immediately took steps that they should work in conjunction with the Radio Direction Finding Stations as soon as tests at Bawdsey were complete. It would be the task of the RDF to detect hostile aircraft whilst still out to sea, then it would be the job of the Observer Corps to track them once they are over land.

But the men of the Observer Corps were much more highly trained under Fighter Command than those of the First World War. Strenuous lectures in aircraft recognition became mandatory, as did lessons in judging aircraft height. Although they were not equipped with any elaborate instruments, it was mainly their enthusiasm, an aircraft recognition booklet, a pair of binoculars and a simple yet effective sighting instrument were the only tools that this dedicated band of men tackled their all important duty.

Once radar, as it had now become known as, had picked up an enemy sighting and the information passed on to the Filter Room at Fighter Command HQ, it was the Group Operations Room that contacted the Observer Corps Command Centre who in turn notified the small Observer Command Posts scattered at between six and ten miles apart along the coastline, where it would be apparent that the detected enemy formation would possibly be sighted. As soon as the call was received, the post, normally manned by three to five men would scan the skies with their binoculars and keep a keen ear out for the sound of aircraft engines. In inclement weather and on days with low cloud, visual sighting was almost an impossibility and detection could only be made by sound. How long they would have to wait to make contact with the enemy, no one knew, all they had been told was "hostile" aircraft had been detected "X miles south of Dover" or wherever the first detection had been made. How old was the message, how fast were the aircraft travelling and how far away were they and on what course. The observers may have to wait half an hour, three quarters, or maybe the aircraft had changed direction, in which case they would approach further up the coast. If possible, any change that had been detected, would come through as a message and the post commander would just say "okay chaps, relax, looks like so and so's got this one," meaning that a post twenty miles along now had the task of visually sighting the enemy.

Once a sighting had been made, the observers had to detect which types of aircraft were in the formation, how many, the heading that they were taking and height. All these factors were of vital importance because it would be the picture that they presented that gave the Sector Stations (Unlike radar stations that gave Fighter Command HQ their sighting and contact first, the Observer Corps gave details of their first sighting to the Sector Station in their area so that fighters could be "scrambled" as soon as possible once the enemy was crossing the coast) an overall view of the situation. Trouble was brewing if the observers gave the height of the enemy as 5,000 feet when in fact they were 8,000 feet, because it meant that when the British fighters were airborne and searching for the enemy, they could easily be "jumped" on by hostile fighter escorts because they had not been at the correct height to meet the formation. The observers would give the type of aircraft detected by its name, Heinkel III, Junkers 88's etc, they did not have to count every single aircraft, this would take up too much valuable time, they had been trained to observe a formation and be able to accurately estimate its strength and they would report this strength as "50 plus" or "100 plus". If any fighter escort could be visually seen, this may be reported, but generally, fighter escorts flew much higher than the bomber formation that they were protecting. But even if a fighter escort was not reported, the Sector Station on receiving the report knew full well that there was one there… there always was.

As you can see, the importance of the Observer Corps was

an extremely important one. Working on information already received, they were the last to provide details of height, location, heading and strength of the enemy before Fighter Command would despatch their fighters to engage combat. They had no sophisticated operation equipment, just experience and simple tools.

As Churchill said, it was like going from the middle of the twentieth century to the early stone age. To cater to this transition there were "Lost Property Offices" which recorded aircraft reported by the Observer Corps but not by radar. (The Observer Corps were only allowed to track aircraft that had been detected by the Radar Stations.)

AIR INTELLIGENCE

Another service that was vital to Fighter Command was those that determined which aircraft were the enemy and which were friendly. Many that have made a study of the Battle of Britain would have heard about what became known as "The Battle of Barking Creek". It was simply the failure to identify fighters of the R.A.F. and hostile enemy aircraft and the result was that three Hurricanes of the R.A.F. were shot down by friendly Spitfires.

One of these methods used to distinguish friendly and enemy aircraft was "Identification Friend or Foe" or IFF as became known. Basically the workings of IFF, was that aircraft of Fighter Command were fitted with a radiating device that would radiate a much stronger signal back than the signal that it received. Air intelligence, on receiving the blips on their screens would see a much stronger blip than normal thus it could then be identified as a friendly aircraft.

The old building, once a stately home then later becoming a school for girls until it gave way to become Bentley Priory the Headquarters of Fighter Command. This was the nerve centre of all operations although many were conducted from the headquarters of the individual Group Headquarters in various parts of the country. It played one of the most important parts during the Battle of Britain to which Bentley Priory will always be associated.

The Radar Stations and the Observer Corps were fine for the purpose of detecting and tracking hostile aircraft coming in from across the English Channel, but to make the detection system work and function properly the it was essential for the Sector Controllers to have an accurate assessment as to the position of their own fighter aircraft. Without knowing where their aircraft were it would have been impossible to vector them to another combat area or where their aircraft were to in relation to any current attack.

One of the early methods of friendly aircraft detection was being experimented as early as February 1939. A.F. Wilkins and a R.H.A. Carter, scientists at Bawdsey were busy testing apparatus that they had built in an effort to display a different sort of blip on the CRT screens so that the filter rooms could tell if a detected

An Observer Corps spotter scans the skies of London.

aircraft was one of theirs, or if it was an enemy aircraft. During one of the official tests in March 1939, the operators at Bawdsey, busy checking their screens suddenly picked up an unusual and strange blip on the screens. Instead of the small round blip that was usually displayed, this one was brighter and the shape was elongated. They had picked up the experimental aircraft that was fitted with a new device and they tracked it for many minutes.

The information was immediately sent to Bentley Priory Filter Room and it was classified as a confirmed detection of a friendly aircraft. One of those present at "Bentley" was Lord Chatfield who was Minister for Co-ordination of Defence who exclaimed that this was a great step forward and that radio detection was about to be perfected. ACM Hugh Dowding was also aware of the contribution that IFF could make in aircraft detection, and by early 1940 with the Battle of Barking Creek in which two Hurricanes of 56 Squadron were accidently shot down by Spitfires of 74 Squadron was still fresh in his mind, he was pushing for such an apparatus where he could know the position of all friendly aircraft.

IFF worked reasonably well but it did have its failings. In dogfights it became impossible to distinguish one aircraft from another. Many times friendly aircraft were not able to be detected while at time they were easily seen.

In practice, the IFF system was later to be found to be not totally reliable, and accurate aircraft identification remained founded on the judgment made at Filter Rooms, where information about aircraft movements of home forces was available.

A later method that was introduced was the use of HF/DF, High Frequency Direction Finding to give it its correct name, but to most it was known as "Pip-squeak" the code name given to the apparatus. All British fighters were equipped with a TR9D transmitter receiver. This was the only contact that a pilot had with ground control, although its main drawback was that it was limited to a range of only 40 - 45 miles (64 - 72Km) at about

15,000 feet (4,545m) although under perfect weather conditions this range could be extended further. The unit had two channels. One channel was used for the purpose of voice communication with Sector Control to which the aircraft was attached. Each squadron had its own frequency and always operated with this setting. The other channel was set on a common frequency to all squadrons and was unsuitable for voice communication. It was this channel that was known as "Pip-squeak".

As soon as this channel was selected, the transmitter sounded a shrill fourteen second whistle at about 1,000 cycles, which was received by the Sector Controller.

Automatic periodic DF transmissions from aircraft were achieved by "pip-squeak" (named for the cartoon characters of the day). It automatically switched on the HF transmitter in the aircraft for 14 seconds every minute. A clock in the control room showed (from four coloured sections) which aircraft should be transmitting (by a hand rotating once a minute).

Each of four aircraft had its position plotted once a minute and navigation was not necessary. If one forgot to switch on, the controller would say "Is your cockerel crowing?" cockerel being the code word for Pip-squeak.

The DF system and radar were the keys to all the interceptions made and meant that it was unnecessary to fly standing patrols (which were impossible anyway). The HF/DF bands were overcrowded and distorted so a VHF (Very High Frequency) Radio Telephony (RT) set with a range of 100 miles was needed.

Alas, the TR (Transmitter Receiver)1143 was not forthcoming in time and the Battle of Britain was fought largely on HF with the old crystal controlled TR9 with which I was still battling as late as 1943!

By September 1940 only 16 day fighter squadrons had VHF.

A sector had three direction finding (D/F) stations that formed a triangle with each corner being approximately thirty miles apart and each being connected by a land line to the stations Fixer Room.

Here, on a small map table, the D/F stations were marked and were surrounded by a compass rose. As each of the D/F stations received its bearing from "Pip-squeak" a plotter at the map table could then take a line, with a humble piece of string from each D/F station on the map, and when that station reported the direction from which it picked up the aircraft's signal, the operator of the string aligned it with that direction. Thus, when the three strings were aligned in unison, where they crossed was the position of the aircraft.

Calculating quickly the compass course on which to send the fighter squadrons for accurate interception proved a vexing problem. Not only were pages of trigonometry consulted but a number of small computers were built to assist the calculation. Until one day, watching an exercise, an exasperated Wing Commander said he could judge the interception course by eye alone. He was immediately challenged to do so by the irritated boffins. He picked up the microphone that connected the Operations Room with the fighter pilots and gave them courses, until two R.A.F. formations taking part in the exercise met in a perfect interception.

The Wing Commander's judgment was greeted by amazed disbelief. Asked to explain how he did it, he said it was a process of imagining an isosceles triangle, with the fighters and bombers at each base corner -- interception would take place at the summit. He gave the course accordingly. It was a rough calculation but quite good enough to become standard procedure. The most common discrepancy, due to the superior speed of the fighters, was no real problem. The fighters were ordered to orbit until the bombers arrived.

- C H A P T E R 1 7 -

THE MEN WHO ALSO SERVE

ANY ACCOUNT of how AA defences developed must include the story of the Royal Observer Corps. This is how its members live and work.

Two men stand in a sand-bagged emplacement built high on a hill to give an unbroken view. The evening is completely quiet, but they are listening hard. The wild fowl on the marsh below have been agitating, and that is often the first hint of a Heinkel.

One man wears head-phones, with a mouthpiece strapped over his chest. The other is working a plotting instrument, which stands on a tripod in the centre of the post. It consists of a round dial, marked with numbers and squares. On top of this is a height finder.

Their observations are reported into the telephone rather as follows: "Seen. 5678. South-east. Eight. At 10,000." This means that they have seen 'planes approaching over the square denoted by 5678 on their charts, that they are headed south-east, that they are eight in number and flying at 10,000 feet. They also report the type of plane. More often than not the 'plane is friendly, but reports are made just the same. The observers can recognise almost any 'plane without thinking twice, and their accuracy at estimating heights is uncannily good.

There are 1,400 of these posts manned by men and women, mostly part-time workers, who give what time they can spare from their normal work. It is not always pleasant, for they cannot take shelter however bad the weather is, nor can they have a fire because it would be seen from the air. Plenty of mistakes can be made. A certain kind of railway-carriage dynamo sounds like a distant air-raid siren, and the hum of a factory or a motor-boat engine can be extraordinarily like the intermittent drone of a 'plane.

The telephone which one of the observers wears connects the post to a centre. Here a crew of men and women sit round a table on which is a large-scale map of the area, broken up into squares and sub-divided into the smaller, numbered squares as at the posts. Each member wears head-phones with a mouth-piece strapped over his chest and is in direct contact with three of the posts.

When a post reports the presence of an aircraft, a coloured counter is put into the appropriate square. As the aircraft is reported to have moved, so the counter follows it.

Above the table, on a platform, are the tellers. Watching the table, they report the movements on the chart to fighter groups, airfields and other defence centres responsible for the reception of the enemy. Friendly and enemy 'planes have different designations, and from a glance at the chart you can see their relative positions. As the raiders move out of the area the neighbouring centres are warned of their approach. Whether you are friend or enemy they are tracking you all the time. The Royal Observer Corps have been on watch night and day without a break since August 24th, 1939.

Another girder of the "Roof Over Britain" is the work of the Royal Corps of Signals. The whole system of defence is based on first-class communications - on telling the gunners what is happening so that they can make arrangements for what is likely to happen somewhere else. The whole AA Command is a network of communication. Each gun and searchlight site is connected with its gun-operations room and its neighbours. Gun and Light sites, observer posts, operations rooms, fighter sectors and airfields are all inter-connected in a maze of telephone cables, supplemented by dispatch riders and radio. The Post Office telephone and telegraph system has been used as a basis. To its thousands of miles of wire, stretching to every corner of the country, have been added hundreds of miles of field lines and new circuits. For each circuit there are alternatives planned in case of emergency. Even the location of private phones is noted, so that, if need be, they can be taken over and used.

When the raids come, the cables are liable to get broken. Then the line parties of the Royal Corps of Signals have to get to work, often in extremely difficult conditions, tracing and repairing the breakdowns. Here is the story of one of these excursions, which happened during the attacks on London. It concerns a certain gun site on the Isle of Dogs.

The line party, consisting of a subaltern, and two trucks each carrying about ten men and loaded with the usual signals paraphernalia - cables, poles, ladders, lengths of spun yarn, climbing irons and cable barrows for paying out cable, got their orders at 9.30 a.m.

It took quite a time to drive down to the Isle of Dogs through all the deviations caused by bombs which had exploded, or were expected to explode.

The Isle of Dogs is not a natural island, but a tongue of land moulded by a U-bend in the Thames and isolated by ramifications of docks. Silhouetted by the river, it was a natural target, and the warehouses and working-class housing which crowded it had taken a terrible battering. The fires were still burning, and across the river the Surrey Docks were burning too.

There was one approach left open by which the signals lorries could approach the gun site, and this was stopped a hundred yards before the site by a large bomb crater. The site was ringed with craters, so it was impossible to get a lorry on to it.

In the ordinary way a line party works its way along the cables, repairing them where they are broken. But the cables to this gun site had been laid mostly underground and partly under water. They had been laid by the G.P.O., who in the ordinary way would be responsible for their maintenance; but, as may be imagined, the G.P.O. were not entirely disengaged that morning. There was no possibility of getting such a complicated job done, and it was urgently necessary to restore communications by nightfall. The only way was to lay an entirely new cable to the nearest telephone exchange, which was two miles away by direct route, and, allowing for diversions, likely to be nearly twice as far.

There was no time to carry the cable properly on poles; they

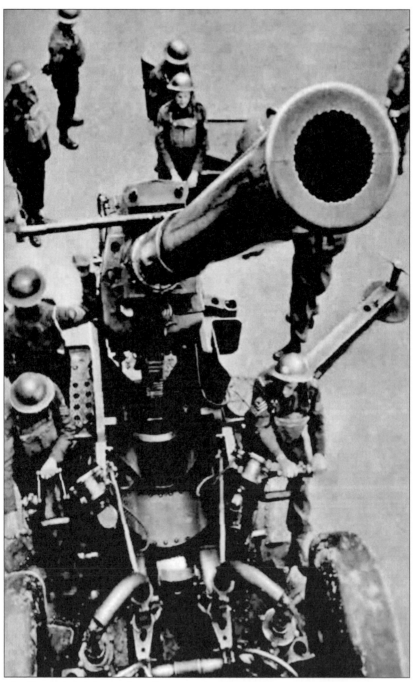

On Target! A 3.7 gun detachment at battle practice. In the foreground, two gunners adjust bearing and elevation as transmitted by the predictor. The Sergeant, back to camera, is ready to give the signal to fire.

had to lay it along the gutter, leaving signalmen at intervals to guard it. It was a hot day, and though the fires were still burning, it was strangely quiet. The streets were deserted, like those of a wild-west ghost town. The little shops were there, with goods in the window but no one in the back room waiting to sell them. Every so often they came to a warehouse on fire and they had to estimate how far to allow for the fire to spread before laying the cable. Mostly they laid it along the gutter, but sometimes over the ruins of a building, and once over the swing bridge of a dock. The sirens went several times, but nothing serious developed. They plodded on, round warehouses, under cranes, across scrap-iron yards, scrub-land, dock-railway lines, under fences, over bridges. The air was laden with smoke, dust and filth. The men were filthy and sweating with the heat and annoyance of having to make constant diversions to avoid delayed-action bombs, which in those days were much more incalculable dangers than they are now.

Working at great pressure the men finally got the line through at 4 p.m. When it came to testing it, they weren't at all sure that it would work. But it did, and just as the voice came through, the sirens announced the first of the night's attacks.

Being a despatch rider isn't much fun during a heavy raid. With the breaking down of communications, despatch riders are overworked taking messages to sites. All the troubles of driving a car through the rubble, clay and water of a bombed area are multiplied many times on a motor bike. You have greater mobility, but much greater discomforts. The compensating factor is that, owing to the acuteness of these discomforts, you quickly lose most of your capacity for apprehension, and develop a certain bitter relish for setbacks.

During the Coventry attacks one D.R., L-Cpl. Sidney Slight, was visiting an ammunition dump when a bomb landed near by and blew him a dozen yards. He recovered his bike and a few minutes later his tyre was burst open by splinters. He exchanged his wheel for one taken from another bike, and musing on what the

141

owner would say when he came to use his bike, he set off again. He drove up one road, and five minutes later made the return journey. An army truck saved him from a nasty spill, for seeing its shape in the darkness he pulled up to avoid it, and found it was wedged in a bomb crater which hadn't been there five minutes before and into which he would have pitched.

A London D.R., Signalman Hoy, was less lucky. He drove into a bomb crater and found himself practically buried in wet slimy clay. A policeman came to help him out and fell in himself, wearing a brand new uniform. Another D.R. fell off his bike 18 times in 40 minutes, and when he arrived, found he was due to go on guard in 35 minutes time.

The other great supporting arm of AA Command is the Royal Army Ordnance Corps, which supplies and maintains all the guns and instruments, all the lights and all the generating sets.

This has been built up from as near nothing as made little difference. When the war started there were only a few sets of hand tools to maintain the AA defences of London. But the R.A.O.C. men not only did their own work, but often-other people's as well. For instance, there was a great shortage of striker pins, which strike the cartridge and detonate the charge. As mass raids were expected to start any time, it was essential that we should be able to fire what shells we had from any guns that had so far been delivered. But there was no way of getting striker pins except for the R.A.O.C. to make them. They did this by rescuing an ancient hand-driven lathe which had been condemned as useless, and working it night and day.

Individual initiative has been the keynote all along. Some R.A.O.C. men were fixing fire-control instruments, which involved taking a cable along a pipe leading through a concrete emplacement. But there was a kink in the pipe too steep to thread the cable through. They solved this problem by borrowing a local ferret and sending it through the pipe with a piece of string tied to one leg and then pulling the cable through at the end of the string.

When the raids started the work of maintenance became urgent and arduous in the extreme. After every substantial engagement the guns and instruments must be examined and checked. This is highly technical work and it means a tremendous amount of work for the limited numbers of R.A.O.C. men.

- C H A P T E R   1 8 -

AIR INTELLIGENCE:
THE EARS OF FIGHTER COMMAND

A NUMBER of methods were used to intercept German messages, all of them becoming the "Ears of Fighter Command". The Royal Air Force relied very heavily on Intelligence reports, and it was these reports that described German troop and infantry movements as well as movements that were within the German *Luftwaffe*. Information regarding German movements and orders were made from at least four main sources. One of these was the Enigma machine. A highly sophisticated machine that was used by the Germans that used code to transmit secret messages, and the code was changed daily.

Where radar was the "Eyes" of Fighter Command, assisting them to see out beyond the coastline and accurately pinpoint formations of enemy aircraft over one hundred miles distant, being able to hear what information was being passed on from German Military Headquarters to the various commanders would have been a bonus. Details of new decisions, military movements, when and where the different commanders would be at different times, when important meetings were being arranged with Hitler and so on. Of course, Britain did have its means of intelligence; both sides had spies often planted in important organisations. But to be able to "hear" commands and instruction moments after they had been given would have been a bonus to the British war effort.

In August 1939, the Polish government gave Britain a German code machine that they had seized when it was sent to the German Legislation in Warsaw, complete with the methods on how any codes being sent could be deciphered. Britain already had one of these machines that had been invented in Holland and a German company took out a patent on the machine in 1923. Acquiring it in 1928 and not knowing too much about the machine, which Britain called the Tippex, and unable to work out its fundamentals, the British put it away and there it remained gathering dust.

The German name for the machine was Enigma, and Britain as well continued to use it by this name although some sources state that it was called Ultra by the British. "Ultra" was actually a codename for messages and intelligence that had been derived from Enigma. Once Britain realised the value of Enigma and how important a part it could play, it was thought that only two commanders in the Royal Air Force, ACM Hugh Dowding and AVM Keith Park knew of its existence other than certain members of the War Office. In actual fact, historian Martin Gilbert has found that because messages were very slow in being deciphered, the information was often 48 hours old before it could have been handed to Fighter Command, and that Fighter Command C-in-C ACM Hugh Dowding did not know of its existence until October 16th 1940 when Dowding was added to the list of people that were made aware of Enigma's existence. In reality, most 'Ultra' decrypts were of limited value during the Battle of Britain, mainly due to the slow deciphering of the machine. The Germans changed the

Enigma machine in use.

rotors of the machine daily which meant that each day the British had to determine which had been changed so that any codes could continue to be broken.

It is a well-known fact that Enigma was of great assistance to the British from 1941 onwards when they were able to decipher the codes more quickly and efficiently. But it is not a proven fact that Enigma was of any assistance to ACM Hugh Dowding. Two historians seem to differ on this fact, and also Martin Gilbert was supposed to have found evidence that Dowding did not know of its existence is mentioned by historian John Ray:

"According to Winterbotham, who was a senior Air Intelligence officer, both Dowding and Park benefited from a foreknowledge of German intentions, a claim supported by historians as eminent as Ronald Lewin and John Terraine. However, the record was set straight by Martin Gilbert, who showed that not until 16 October 1940 was the C-in-C added to the list of those privy to Enigma. Hinsley states of Enigma, "the deductions were of no operational value to the C-in-C, Fighter Command," and that Dowding had to depend on "his own strategic judgement," without help." - John Ray, Battle of Britain - New Perspectives, p59, Arms & Armour Press 1994.

We could compare the above with Richard Townshend Bickers, who based his information on Enigma on the reports of Group Captain F.W. Winterbotham who was the man in charge of Enigma:

"The Germans had called their first cyphering machine 'Enigma' and the British gave this name to all German cyphers. 'Ultra' was the British codename for intelligence derived from Enigma and other machine cyphers. The only two commanders in the R.A.F. who knew of Enigma and Ultra were Dowding and No. 11 Group's Air Vice Marshal Keith Park. A specific instance of its importance in the Battle of Britain was that the heavy air raids on August 15, 1940 did not take these two senior officers by surprise. The information given to them was precise: *Luftflotten* 2, 3 and 5 would make the attacks, which were timed to keep the defenders at full stretch throughout the day. F. W. Winterbotham, who, as a group captain, was responsible for Ultra, recorded that Dowding told him that it was of the greatest help to him to know what Goering's policy was and enabled him to use his fighter squadrons with the greatest possible economy." - Richard Townshend Bickers, Battle of Britain, p59 Salamander 1999.

So, did Enigma help Dowding on August 15th 1940 as Winterbotham stated in Bickers book? If this is true, then why didn't Enigma help Dowding when Kenley and Biggin Hill aerodromes were taken by surprise on August 18th 1940. And why didn't Enigma help Dowding when London was attacked on September 7th 1940. If they knew that an attack was to be made on London, why did Dowding ask AVM Keith Park to leave 11 Group HQ and join him in a conference at Fighter Command HQ.

On these theories, we can only be led to believe that the writings of John Ray are the more correct, which in turn means that Dowding did not have access to Enigma, and further to that, Intelligence had still not been able to efficiently interpret and decipher the German codes accurately during the time of the Battle of Britain.

CHAPTER 19

LISTENING IN TO GERMANY
BY RADIO

IT BECAME apparent to R.A.F. Intelligence that not all transmitted broadcasts would be in code. It was unclear as to what transmissions would be sent in Morse code and what would be sent by the spoken word. Whichever way it was, if R.A.F. Intelligence could pick up German transmissions it would most certainly be of valuable assistance and there was always the possibility that Germany would give away vital pieces of information that would allow the R.A.F. to know of every move the *Luftwaffe* would be making.

The organisation that was responsible for radio intelligence was known as the Y Service. They would listen in to spoken word messages as well as coded messages that were sent to the Government Code and Cypher School at Bletchley Park. These messages were to provide information as to *Luftwaffe* strength, proposed attacks and various movements. All this information acquired by the Y Service was sent to Air Intelligence at the Air Ministry. Quite often messages were picked up from E-boats out to sea, although this information was of little use to the Air Ministry, they passed all German naval intercepted messages on to the Admiralty.

In the first three months of the war, the only messages picked up were in Morse using the W/T (Wireless telegraphy) method. It was soon realised that ham radio operators were picking up voice messages which they could not understand on the 40 megacycle band using R/T (Radio telegraphy). R.A.F. Intelligence purchased some American Hallicrafter 510 units that could pick up the 40 megacycle band, and by March 1940, had them set them up at Hawkinge Kent. Almost immediately they commenced to pick up German radio transmissions. The only problem was that they seemed to have overlooked the fact that Germans actually speak the German language, and no one in the R.A.F. at Hawkinge spoke or understood the language. It has been said that luckily, an AA gun operator with the army stationed on the base did understand German so he was quickly transferred into the R.A.F. and operated a radio instead of an anti-aircraft gun.

Within the next couple of months, the R.A.F. went on a recruiting campaign from within the Womens Auxiliary Air Service (WAAFs) in an effort to find personnel who not only understood German, but who had actually lived in Germany because they would have a better understanding of the various dialects. By the beginning of the Battle of Britain, six or seven women had been found and were working as Intelligence Operators from a new base at Fairlight in Sussex.

The WAAFs picked up the R/T messages very quickly and German call signs became very familiar. They listened in to *Luftwaffe* pilots having conversation with each other and soon it was realised that German aircrew had no respect for secrecy and often would mention the number of aircraft that would be in the formation and in many cases let their destination slip.

This information was invaluable to R.A.F. Intelligence, and it was not long before the Air Ministry realised the contribution that these 'listening posts' were providing to the war effort, that following requests from other 'Groups' within Fighter Command, more branches of the Y Service were set up in 10 Group at Street in Devon, in 12 Group at Gorleston in Norfolk, and for 13 Group at Scarborough in Yorkshire. 11 Groups 'listening post' at Fairlight was moved to West Kingsdown in Kent and became the headquarters of the Home Defence Unit as it now became officially known as.

CHAPTER 20

DOWDING & BENTLEY PRIORY

"To him, the people of Britain and the people of the Free World owe largely the way of life and the liberties they enjoy today."
The closing words on Dowding's statue.

WHENEVER WE think of the Battle of Britain, our thoughts turn to Fighter Command, if we thought of Fighter Command, our thoughts would then turn to Air Chief Marshal Lord Hugh Dowding, and if we thought of Hugh Dowding we would then think of the nerve centre of Fighter Command, Bentley Priory.

It was in July 1936, that during a complete reorganisation of the Royal Air Force, the task of creating an all new section fell to Air Marshal Sir Hugh Caswell Tremenhere Dowding KCB. This section was to be known as Fighter Command. Dowding had had an impeccable career that had originated in 1900 as an Army Subaltern with the Royal Garrison Artillery and it continued with the Royal Flying Corps during the First World War. He had commanded Fighting Area in the earlier Air Defence of Great Britain (ADGB) organisation in 1929-30 and thereafter for six years he was employed as Air Member for Research and Development on the Air Council. He was a man who had faith in the Radio Direction Finding (RDF) later to become known as Radar of which he had great influence on its future development.

Dowding was a man of strong character with a mind capable of deep thought and foresight, and had very positive views on how his new Command and the air defence system should develop. He was of a naturally reserved nature with a disinclination towards most forms of socialising; his seemingly humorless, often grumpy image portrayed to those not of close acquaintance, plus a facility of quick acid comment, gave him enemies and a reputation for being difficult. He sought the favour of no one. From his early service days the nickname 'Stuffy' endured.

Dowding was given Bentley Priory as his headquarters. It was to be the nerve centre of Fighter Command. It was back in March 1926 that the Royal Air Force acquired a rather dilapidated house and land in Stanmore that is now known as Bentley Priory. On 26 May it became Headquarters of Inland Area that administered a number of air force home establishments and was under the command of Air Vice-marshal Tom Webb-Bowen CB, CMG. But before this, the 'Priory' had an interesting, yet chequered history. Originally, a rather insignificant small house that was owned by a Mr. James Duberly it had been renovated, with the addition of many additional rooms that greatly increased its size, and became a highly prestigious country estate in the possession of The Hon James John Hamilton. In 1789 as 9th Earl and First Marquess of Abercorn, he engaged the services of architect Sir John Sloane to carry out massive extensions to the house and buildings at considerable cost. Later, it was owned by builder Sir John Kelp and when a Mr. Frederick Gordon took over the elegant buildings and land it was turned into a luxurious private hotel. Before much of the property was sold off it had been used as a private boarding school for young ladies before the Royal Air Force acquired it in 1936.

Prior to the official installation of Fighter Command at Bentley Priory, discussions were taking place on the functions of a Command Headquarters Operations Room would be expected to fulfil. On 10 June Dowding attended a high level meeting held to lay down the basic requirement for the room and its associated communications. It was concluded that all intelligence on aircraft in flight supplied by the various observation sources, including Radar, should be transmitted through the most direct channels to Group Headquarters and Sector airfields. It was thought that it might be necessary for the long-range readings from the proposed Radar stations on the coast to be initially transmitted direct to Bentley Priory and plotted on a large map there; maps at Groups or Sectors would basically show only the Group's area of responsibility. Reports from Secret Services sources and enemy radio interceptions would normally be of a strategic nature and, as such would be passed on to Fighter Command and not directly to Groups. The Admiralty should have a direct link with the air defence system through Fighter Command.

Prior to moving into Bentley Priory, Dowding lived and conducted his affairs from his home at Wimbledon Hill in the south west of London, and it was from here that he outlined his plans for setting up an Operations Room at the 'Priory'.

In July 1936 Dowding made his first visit to Bentley Priory, HQ of the newly created Fighter Command. Bentley Priory was an old gothic house on a hill to the extreme northwest of London. It was typical of this idiosyncratic man that instead of arranging the ceremony that would normally take place, he arrived at nine-o'clock in the morning unannounced and all alone. The guard was extremely reluctant to let him through the gate but after inspecting his papers, he handed him over to the most senior man there, a sergeant from the Orderly Room. The two men wandered through the grounds and then through the empty rooms. Selecting a room with a southerly view, Dowding asked the sergeant to put his name on the door, thanked him and left.

"The Ball Room seems to be most suitable for the purpose although this of course may not be desirable as a permanent location owing to the fact the Priory is extremely conspicuous from the air and the rooms would be very difficult to render gas proof. I do, however, wish to make a start immediately so that the delay in the production of my permanent Operations Room may be reduced to a minimum and only by immediate experiment can be determined the requirements necessary for the purpose."

Dowding went to say that in the centre of the Ball Room would be the main Operations Room Table that would be covered by a huge map that would cover from Edinburgh in the north to the

French coast, and from the border of Wales in the west to the east of Belgium. A viewing gallery would be required along the North and West sides of the Ball Room so that it would be possible to observe the various movements that would be displayed on the map below. Also, teleprinters would have to be installed, and these would be placed in the Rotunda.

An intricate telephone and communication system would have to be installed. What was happening around the British coastline would be clearly displayed on the huge map that occupied the ballroom. Reports from the long-distance radar could possibly be received direct, and then relayed to the Groups Headquarters. Any Intelligence information would most certainly be received first at Bentley Priory and then circulated to groups and military offices. Finally, all movements of enemy and friendly bombers would be tracked and displayed on the map, but possibly for reasons of not making the mapboard to complicated and messy, friendly fighter movements would not be shown. A series of lights would be installed on one of the walls, and these would indicate as to the state of readiness of fighter groups.

"To me, an LAC, Air Chief Marshal Dowding lived in a different world. His personal clerk was one Corporal Custance and when he went on leave I had the privilege of being his 'stand-in'. Apart from being called upon to take down pages of shorthand upon highly secret fighter defence matters, I have little recollection of the Air Chief Marshal, except that he was stern but kind. Of the other Officers, in those days 95% were of the General Duties Branch and all were pilots, each having to perform a number of flying hours per year."

The pre-1939 R.A.F. Officer was most emphatically an Officer and a gentleman and, as such, had Service and social obligations. The more senior ones were ex RFC or RNAS. The only time we saw any of our Officers in uniform was when they were going on a Staff visit, Armistice Day, Kings Birthday or other such occasion; normally they came to work in lounge suits. Headquarters Units were not commanded by a Commanding Officer but by a Camp Commandant and ours was one Flight Lieutenant Gearing.

Looking back, I can only say that at Bentley Priory we were an extremely happy set of people; I cannot recall any unpleasant words or deeds. Esprit-de-Corps and morale were of the highest order. In the very stable and civilised conduct of affairs in the United Kingdom at that time security was almost unnecessary, but there was always a Duty Staff Officer, a Duty Clerk, Duty Signals Personnel and an Air Ministry civilian policeman or two on duty.

Leading Aircraftman Jim Griffiths went on to say that, as an LAC his weekly pay was 31/6d of which a 10/6d of that was placed in a Post Office Savings Account. He enjoyed life at Bentley Priory, and he had many memorable times playing sports, the odd dance at the NAAFI and visits to theatres and pubs. Occasionally he received weekend leave which he spent mostly with his parents although he did have a good relationship with his girlfriend. At Bentley Priory, he had his own room unlike other LAC's on station who had to live a barrack room lifestyle, and the food at Bentley was absolutely first class. There was an odd parade but there was also a lot of hard work that was generally spread over long hours.

Work on the Experimental Operations Room was sufficiently advanced by 11th December 1939, that Dowding wrote to the Air Ministry requesting the installation of GPO telephone lines. He also made mention of the intention to limit the field of experiment to a single link up with No.11 (Fighter) Group, and in so doing, concentrating effort in developing and proving a prototype component of the future organisation.

Hugh Dowding in his role as Chairman of the Home Defence Committee's Sub Committee in May 1937, which was also the date of the creation of No.12 Fighter Group, gave a lecture to members of the R.A.F. Staff College on "Fighter Command in Home Defence". and when we look at the basis of Dowding's lecture, we are to find that his ideas and opinions were remarkably prophetic.

Sir Hugh Dowding and an aide with several Battle of Britain fighter pilots outside the Air Ministry in London during the celebration of the second anniversary of the RAF's most successful day of the Battle. Left to right: Sqn Ldr A C Bartley DFC, Wg Cdr D F B Sheen DFC, Wg Cdr I R Gleed DSO DFC, Wg Cdr Max Aitken DSO DFC, Wg Cdr A G Malan DSO DFC, Sqn Ldr A C Deere DFC, Air Chief Marshal Sir Hugh Dowding, Flt Off E C Henderson, Flt Lt R H Hilary, Wg Cdr J A Kent DFC AFC, Wg Cdr C B F Kingcome, Sqn Ldr D H Watkins DFC and WO R H Gretton.

Hugh Dowding first spoke about how a war would be most quickly lost and stated that this might possibly be caused by indiscriminate air attacks on London and creating panic amongst its population. As an alternative, an immediate paralysis of the food supply would have exactly the same effect and that if the country could be secured against a quick decision of this kind, then the only defeat could come from the slower process of exhaustion of equipment, personnel, food, raw materials, sea transport and other resources. He went on to state that the focal point of the machinery of Government and the main centre for the distribution of the countries food supplies would be London itself, and concluded that the most important task would therefore be the defence of London itself.

The most important task therefore would be that defending London would be the most important task in the defence of Great Britain. Dowding went on to say, that if he was the dictator, then first and foremost, he would destroy the enemy's Air Force at his airfields, reserve storage depots and factories etc.

Dowding continued:

"There is another possible form of attack which I think deserves closer study than it has received up to the present. I refer to the attacks on our food and supply ships at sea."

He went on to say that the diversion of shipping away from the vulnerable areas of the Port of London and the Thames Estuary, to western ports be a matter of highest importance, his concern was the possibility of attacks on inland targets becoming unsustainable and that the bulk of offensive power being turned to supply ships at sea.

He went on:

"It seems to me that our shipping will, broadly speaking, be as open to submarine attack as it was in the last war and that it will now have to face the additional danger of attack from the air."

On attacks on London, Dowding said that the main dangers would be fire, bomb explosion and gas, and it would probably occur in that order. He considered incendiary attacks on property, that would enable the enemy to utilise for purposes of destruction be the greatest danger that the population would have to face, that a single bomber might distribute a thousand small incendiary bombs, and with a dense population as the city of London a single bomber could initiate something like a hundred small fires.

"There is a serious danger that groups of individual fires, which are not properly dealt with, will unite and cause conflagration which will be beyond the control of any fire fighting organisation which we are likely to be able to provide" he said.

Remember that this was a speech that Dowding gave in 1937.

Dowding had a strong interest in radar, he believed that radar was to be the eyes of Britain's defence system. It is understandable then, that it was of great importance to Dowding that he had direct communications with radar stations from Bentley Priory. Over the last few years radar had improved by research and by trials. Dowding had faith in radar.

It was at Orfordness in 1935 that radar had expanded to such a degree that further accommodation was required. Land was purchased at Bawdsey Manor near Felixstowe on the Suffolk coast, and here although the research team was quite small, the quality, variety and inventiveness was remarkable. By April 1937, they were engaged in radar trials endeavoring to locate aircraft flying on pre-arranged courses over the North Sea. The results were said to be confused and disappointing and Dowding thought that the general standard of information was as yet unacceptable for his Operations Rooms. Nevertheless, by August the same year a plan for the construction of coastal radar stations had already been agreed.

Radar stations were already in operation at Orfordness, Bawdsey and Canewdon, and two others at Great Bromley and Dunkirk had yet to be completed. But by August 1937 it was decided to go ahead with the whole chain, making twenty in all. The probable average cost of each of the new stations would be:

Purchase of land - £ 3,000

Construction of towers - £28,000

Power, electrical distribution, stand-by-plant etc - £ 8,000

Operational buildings - £ 3,000

Roads, paths and fencing - £ 5,000

Quarters for two warders - £ 1,200

Contingencies - £ 3,800

Total - £52,000

The fifteen additional stations would cost £780,000. For more powerful apparatus for each of the 20 stations @ £16,000 it would cost £320,000 in all. The total cost of the chain would be £1,305,000. The annual operating cost was estimated at £174,000. The Treasury gave sanction to the proposal on 13th August 1937. - Dowding and Headquarters Fighter Command/Peter Flint p209 Appendix 3

Each of these would have four receiver masts that would be 250 feet high and four transmitter masts with each one being 350 feet high. The reason for duplication was their vulnerability to air attack, and the likelihood that transmissions would be interfered with or 'jammed' by the Germans. In the event of a mast or its aerials being damaged, or operating frequency being impaired, there were others that were ready to take over. To improve results they would be sited close enough together to form a chain where each station oversaw part of its neighbours detection area.

Radar was in the hands of both civilian scientists and R.A.F. Signals specialists, and after studying the results of the unsatisfactory trials in April 1937, Squadron Leader Raymond Hart was to become very influential in the study of radar operations. With other members of the team they agreed that if the radar stations were sited close enough together, then there would be an overlap in their fields of observation, which this would make it possible for every part of the coast to be watched. Although the technique made things complicated, it did require very careful handling and correlation of readings from two adjacent stations, but this method allowed the stations to be linked like a chain along the coastline. The system was approved by Dowding who, from early in the peace had great faith in radar and progress was being made with correlated information from the radar stations being relayed directly to the Bentley Priory Filter Rooms.

Air Chief Marshal Hugh Dowding was to stay at Bentley Priory for the duration of the Battle of Britain and until he was relieved of his position as AOC Fighter Command. The 'Priory' was constantly in use throughout the rest of the war and today stands as a monument to the operations that were conducted there that finally led to victory in WWII.

- CHAPTER 21 -
THE FIRST WINTER

AT 9.20 in the morning of October 16th, 1939, the Gun Operations Room in the Forth Area started to record the approach of enemy aircraft. All the morning these plots continued, the aircraft flying very high and obviously out on reconnaissance. When they were seen by gun crews, which was rarely, they were too high to be positively identified, and as they were only isolated 'planes, no fire was opened. At twenty-seven minutes past two that afternoon, operators in the Forth Gun Operations Room were astonished to see a red light flash up, meaning "Guns in Action." No warning of any sort had been received, and no sirens had sounded. They immediately sent out the order "Action" to all sites, and almost at that moment enemy aircraft appeared over the Forth Bridge. No attempt was made to bomb the bridge itself; the Germans were trying for two warships lying near it, and for another coming up the Forth. A gun site south of the Forth was busily engaged in gun drill when suddenly the spotters saw what was unmistakably a German aircraft approaching the Forth Bridge. Hurriedly the crew changed their dummy ammunition for live, while their instruments were laid on the 'planes. Before they could open fire it had dived too low, but another had appeared from the clouds. This time the gunners were more fortunate and shot a large portion of the Nazi's tail-plane down into the Firth of Forth. This raider was finished off by a Spitfire, and crashed into the sea off Port Seton. This Heavy AA Battery was the first Anti-Aircraft Battery to help in bringing down an enemy raider over this country.

Meanwhile, all neighbouring gun sites were hurriedly going into action. The raiders, between six and nine in number, flew over from the coast well to the south of their target, at heights of 12,000-15,000 feet. They then turned north, and making good use of cloud cover, descended to about 4,000 feet before diving on their target. All the attacks were made independently and from different directions. After their dive attack they would fly off as low as 50 feet, making it impossible for the heavy gunners to continue firing. In spite of this another plane was damaged by AA fire and our fighters accounted for two more.

Meanwhile a report had come in that a number of biplanes, said to be Henschel 123s, were off the coast near Dunbar; probably a ruse to draw off our fighters.

For nearly two hours on and off the attack continued, until, soon after four o'clock the last of the raiders disappeared, pursued by our fighters. No bombs fell on land or on the dockyard, but a few casualties and some slight damage were suffered by the ships.

Lessons were learned from this raid, which was the first chance of trying out the effect of anti-aircraft fire and fighters in action together. The fighters reported that the bursts of anti-aircraft fire were of great assistance in locating the enemy. Gunners found that the great superiority in speed of the Spitfire over a German bomber made it difficult to know when to stop firing at an enemy 'plane being pursued by a Spitfire.

So our Ack-Ack gun crews, not altogether displeased with their day's work, and well content with being the lucky ones to draw first blood, collected their empty shell cases and hoped the enemy would return.

The Shetlands were the first part of the British Isles to be bombed and there was a song to celebrate the event. The title of the song, "Run, Rabbit, Run," referred to the only casualty sustained during the raid. It was clear that some AA defence was required - though not, of course, for the rabbits, which already had shelters.

The guns landed one mild day in January 1940. Battery headquarters was established and the guns were sent immediately to their sites in a remote corner of the island some 30 miles away. The crews settled down in what accommodation they could find, and started to dig their gun positions by day and think of ways of keeping out the cold by night.

Before their arrival the Germans had come frequently, so they had high hopes of almost daily action. Nothing of the kind occurred. There was one raid soon after arrival, but no more for many weeks. This is recorded merely as a coincidence, but to the Shetlanders it's much more. The gunners' prestige soared.

Most of the gunners were Yorkshiremen, with a sprinkling of young Scots. They were short of men and there was no question of leave, not even a few hours in Lerwick.

The local people depended for their living on Shetland wool. The women walked along carrying great baskets of peat on their backs and knitting all the time. At night the gunners would go into the cottages and drink tea. The Northern Lights were magnificent: the men could have read the newspapers at midnight if they had had any newspapers.

The social event of the week on each site was the visit of an E.N.S.A. Film Unit. It was a godsend to everybody. The apparatus was rigged up in a hut, and the shows were open to Shetlanders. They came from miles around, by every possible means of conveyance except Shetland ponies, of which there seemed to be very few. Many of the islanders had never seen a film before and never seen a train. Afterwards they would push back the benches, sprinkle French chalk on the floor, and dance to music from the Film Unit's sound apparatus. Most of the Shetlanders only knew their own reels, but the gunners soon introduced them to the cultural advances of the mainland.

Probably the temperature in Shetland was no lower than on the mainland. It was the wind that made it so bitter. There were times when it was impossible to stand up.

Like all AA units, they had the problem of how to fill spare time in the evenings, when the work was finished, but they were tied down to the site. In some ways this is an easier matter in really lonely places than it is when the men are tantalisingly near the amenities of a big town but might as well be in the Shetlands for all the chance there is of getting to them. On really lonely sites the gunners know they must provide their own entertainment and so settle down to when suddenly the spotters saw what was unmistakably a German aircraft approaching the Forth Bridge. Hurriedly the crew changed their dummy ammunition for live, while their instruments were laid on the 'planes. Before they could open fire it had dived too low, but another had appeared from the clouds. This time the gunners were more fortunate and shot a large portion of the Nazi's tail-plane down into the Firth of Forth. This raider was finished off by a Spitfire, and crashed into the sea off Port Seton. This Heavy AA Battery was the first Anti-Aircraft Battery to help in bringing down an enemy raider over this country.

Meanwhile, all neighbouring gun sites were hurriedly going into action. The raiders, between six and nine in number, flew over from the coast well to the south of their target, at heights of 12,000-15,000 feet. They then turned north, and making good use of cloud cover, descended to about 4,000 feet before diving on their target. All the attacks were made independently and from different directions. After their dive attack they would fly off as low as 50 feet, making it impossible for the heavy gunners to continue firing. In spite of this another plane was damaged by AA fire and our fighters accounted for two more.

Meanwhile a report had come in that a number of biplanes, said to be Henschel 123s, were off the coast near Dunbar; probably a ruse to draw off our fighters.

For nearly two hours on and off the attack continued, until, soon after four o'clock the last of the raiders disappeared, pursued by our fighters. No bombs fell on land or on the dockyard, but a few casualties and some slight damage were suffered by the ships.

Lessons were learned from this raid, which was the first chance of trying out the effect of anti-aircraft fire and fighters in action together. The fighters reported that the bursts of anti-aircraft fire were of great assistance in locating the enemy. Gunners found that the great superiority in speed of the Spitfire over a German bomber made it difficult to know when to stop firing at an enemy 'plane being pursued by a Spitfire.

So our Ack-Ack gun crews, not altogether displeased with their days work, and well content with being the lucky ones to draw first blood, collected their empty shell cases and hoped the enemy would return.

The Shetlanders were glad to welcome the gunners. Not all communities are so enthusiastic. Take the case of a certain Searchlight Battery - neither typical nor extraordinary. A searchlight site was erected about half a mile from a village, and the inhabitants, partly farmers, partly miners, were perturbed. They had never been bombed and they felt that with the arrival of the searchlights they very well might be. So they held an indignation meeting and sent a letter of protest to the War Office. To aggravate matters, the only billet that could be found for the troops, until their huts were built, was the village hall where all the social events were normally held. But the men were determined, by their behaviour, to fight this hostility and they did so to such purpose that, instead of pursuing their protest to the War Office, the villagers gave them a twelve-guinea wireless set. In no time at all the troop clerk became engaged to the daughter of the local policeman, and when the huts were finished the villagers sent presents of furniture.

Shortly after, the expected bomb did fall. It was not a big one, and it did not land on the village: it landed about 100 yards from the site, where it made quite a mess of the cookhouse. Nobody was hurt, but next morning the entire village turned out to see if any help was needed.

Then the battery was moved a matter of 50 miles. Another protest meeting was held, another letter sent to the War Office, this time protesting against the removal. But it was as much in vain as the first one. However, the link was not broken. The village hired a coach, travelled the 50 miles, taking comforts, cigarettes, etc., and a party was held at the new site.

One Searchlight Battery, made up largely of townsmen, found their first war-station to be in one of the most isolated parts of Britain, on the bleak, lonely Derbyshire peaks. They arrived in icy, snowy weather in a tiny village which consisted of one street, about 90 inhabitants and a handful of houses.

The village was on top of a hill so steep that it took only 20 minutes to walk down it to the nearest real village, but 55 minutes of hard walking to get back. A five-mile route march, once a week, was necessary in order to have a bath.

The site which the troops had to build was four miles away from the village where the men were billeted. This necessitated a march every morning with picks, spades and wheelbarrow. Although the site was so high, no sign of human habitation could be seen except an occasional lonely farmhouse. The men were cheered up to discover that opposite there site was what seemed a flourishing farm. But from the start the farmer put up a "Not Welcome" front; he would not even let them have water with which to make tea - not, at least, till urgent representations had been put over by the troop officer.

The farmer also thought that the arrival of the troops would bring bombing. It was pointed out to him that, if he happened to be right, he would probably need the help of the very men he was antagonising, and, grudging, he saw sense.

During that very severe winter of Christmas, 1940, there was a long period during which it was impossible to get fresh rations to the snowed-up troops. They had to make do on iron rations. But, thanks to a good troop officer they didn't miss one mail. Through blizzards, rainstorms, snow, sleet and hail he rode his motorcycle to and from headquarters, some 30 miles away. Being an officer under these conditions is an arduous, unglamorous job, but a tremendously valuable one. His personality and conduct can make all the difference between philosophical endurance and discontent.

The first winter was not easy. Snow fell early in December, and about Christmas time a frost set in which held until well into February. All over the country there was great inconvenience. To give a typical example, a dozen men at a Light AA site in the Basingstoke area were isolated for three days. The ration truck could not get to them nor could the mobile water unit, and it is extraordinary how- much snow you have to melt to get enough water for shaving. Over in Norfolk there were gales which drove the snow into drifts, sometimes 15 feet deep. The ration trucks found themselves driving across fields - not that it made much difference where they drove, since there was no prospect of reaching their destinations, Wooden boxes were collected and runners made for them, partly out of bits of old pram, partly with bent steel. The rations were loaded on and pulled three or four miles across fields. Coal was carried in sandbags.

Not even the weather could hold up necessary movements of units, such as the sending of special protection to areas which might be in special danger. Here is an idea of what conditions on one such move were like, taken from an officer's diary.

"10th January, 1940. These damn guns were wallowing all over the place. I stood up the entire day, looking backward at the convoy mostly, sometimes looking forwards, but usually with my heart in my mouth wondering how long it would be till something happened. We got to our destination at 18.30 hours. I gave some of the men a rum ration. Riding on top of open vehicles the cold was beyond belief, it would have gone through anything. On the way we passed hundreds and hundreds of duck, mostly teal and mallard, all over the road and railway line; we really had a difficult time to get them out of the way - poor brutes, I suppose it was cold and hunger. Physically I like to think I am fairly hard - I have been cold before, and hellish cold too, but never in my life have I met anything like this. When we stopped it was difficult to stand, so we were glad to push on, contact with the ice seemed more remote when we were moving."

- C H A P T E R   2 2 -

ANTI-AIRCRAFT WOMEN

THIS ACCOUNT cannot end without some description of a highly successful experiment, which has caught the public fancy more than most other developments of AA organisation. This is the introduction of women to form mixed batteries. The first German plane to be shot down by a mixed battery crashed in the Newcastle area on December 8th, 1941. When hit it was a couple of miles away and going out to sea. It was the first proof of a remarkable experiment, the operational significance of which has been obscured by its human interest as well as by a wide range of prejudice.

The first point to bear in mind about women on gun stations is that they are not trained for fun, but because the enemy is at the gates. It is not a whimsical experiment, but a necessary operational plan. The AA Command, in common with other services, have a fixed figure which is their man-power ceiling. There are not enough men to go round now, and as the AA defences are almost continually increasing, the problem gets more and more difficult.

As early as 1938 General Pile invited Miss Caroline Haslett, the woman engineer, to inspect a battery in the Surrey Hills so that she could give her opinion about women's capacity to do the work. She spent several Sundays there and assured the General that women could do the job. The event has proved her right. Women man everything except the guns themselves in Heavy AA units, and man them extremely well. They have the right delicacy of touch, the keenness and the application which is necessary to the somewhat tiresome arts of knob-twiddling which are the lot of the instrument numbers. In principle, also, women will take on all the duties of searchlight detachments. Here again experience has shown that they can be first-class on the job. The first battery started training in spring, 1940. The A.T.S. members were picked from volunteers, and the men 'were newly joined recruits, the point being that men who had known no other army life would not find the atmosphere of a mixed battery hysterically unorthodox. There was considerable anxiety as to how men and women would work together, but there need not have been. They took each other very much for granted; there was none of the musical-comedy-chorus atmosphere which had been anticipated, partly, no doubt, because such men and women had been working side by side in civilian life for years.

For the outside observer one of the most whimsical features of the whole affair was just this matter of fact atmosphere. The idea of men and women marching, eating, drilling and working together - all this under the auspices of the British army - was not without a certain revolutionary tinge. In a mixed battery, women drive and service the trucks, act as sentries and despatch riders, and, in fact, do everything except fire the guns. Broadly speaking, the men. are left with the heavier and dirtier work; but even this has not led to sex-antagonism. Human nature is not always as ungenerous as cynics claim; far from resenting the A.T.S., the men in the mixed batteries show a very real pride in the girls work and are the first to defend them against their critics. One of the most convincing arguments for this experiment is that, the more people have to do with it, the more enthusiastic about it they become.

But we are jumping ahead of the story. In the first mixed battery, as in subsequent batteries, there were more than 200 women and nearly 200 men. Men officers and senior N.C.Os. from established batteries combined with A.T.S. officers to form the nucleus of control. In a mixed battery there are eleven men officers and three A.T.S. officers. The women officers concentrate upon welfare and administration; they have nothing to do with the operational side. Operationally the A.T.S. are entirely under the control of male officers, though the latter have no disciplinary powers except that of reporting the girl concerned to her officer. This naturally produces complications, but they have not proved insoluble.

Messing presented certain problems. The new life made these young women very hungry, and the A.T.S. ration was smaller than the men's. Pending an official decision on this point great care-was necessary to use the available food to the best advantage. By mutual consent the rations for men and women were pooled and shared equally. The women were well represented on the messing committees. After a while appetites were stabilized, and diet was balanced to provide food popular with both sexes. Special regard was paid to the women's need for fresh fruit, salads and milk foods; and a balance was found between this and the spotted dog and cheese and pickles beloved of the old soldier - or the new soldier, for that matter.

Naturally this experiment had its troubles, in that nothing so fundamental could be expected to develop without them. But the women surprised their instructors in many ways. In due course they went to finish their initial training at a practice firing camp. The first shooting was more than encouraging. All types of fire control, on all types of heavy equipment were practiced, with consistently encouraging results. Here is a practice camp report on a mixed battery, not on the first one where personnel were picked with more than usual care, but an ordinary run-of-the-mill battery. The officer who made it out had an ample basis of comparison. In the previous twenty months he had tested more than a hundred batteries including six mixed batteries: and this is his routine report on one of them. Other mixed batteries have had better reports : the particular virtue of this one is that it is typical.

"Bad weather for the first half of the period slowed up progress, but during the latter half considerable improvement was made. The battery is considered fit for operational service on the equipment they will use...

"Predictor bearing and angle drill was good, but particular! laying and fuse prediction need practice. Personnel tests should be frequently carried out and the results carefully analysed. Several individual numbers need intensive training, or weeding out, in order that an otherwise good detachment will not be spoilt...

"There is some good material in this battery among the rank and file, both male and female. They have worked hard and made good progress. The turn-out and marching of both men and girls was of a high order. There is an excellent spirit throughout."

In the late summer of 1941 the first of the Mixed Batteries, having completed its initial three-months' training, was sent to an operational site near London and took over its fighting equipment. For the first time women served with men on a war gun-site. Maintenance of equipment had been a point of some pride during training but with the unit's own equipment a very high standard was set. Soldiers necessarily live hard. Living hard does not mean living uncomfortably, but the soldier relies largely on his own initiative for those comforts he enjoys. In the static life shared by the A.T.S. these considerations do not apply with quite the same force, and although all must keep completely fit, a measure of comfort such as is unobtainable in a mobile theatre can be and is achieved.

Socially the experiment was turning out a great success. The question was how would the women turn out in action? Gunners firing in action for the first time are inwardly excited but outwardly tense and cool. Would the women be?

Well, the officer commanding the first mixed battery to bring down a German 'plane said, "As an old soldier, if I were offered the choice of commanding a mixed battery or a male battery, I say without hesitation I would take the mixed battery. The girls cannot be beaten in action, and in my opinion they are definitely better than the men on the instruments they are manning. Beyond a little natural excitement which only shows itself in rather humorous and quaint remarks, they are quite as steady if not steadier than the men. They are amazingly keen at going into action, and although they are not supposed to learn to use the rifle they are as keen .is anything to do so."

This is by no means an isolated reaction. Of course, the novelty has not worn off yet, but the fact emerges that mixed batteries are a very practical proposition.

WOMEN ON SEARCHLIGHTS

In April 1941, a searchlight site was manned with A.T.S. under experimental training to see whether they were capable of taking over from men. There were 54 A.T.S., aged from 19 to 35, average age 24. The first three weeks were spent in preparing for the relatively hard, open-air life on a searchlight site. There was much drill and P.T., and five route marches; also instruction in map reading, anti-gas drill and aircraft recognition. Then came a month's technical training, at the end of which everyone passed the tests: the standard reached was higher than that of most men operating searchlights.

On all except six days, from April 24th to June 19th, there were no sick. The highest number of sick was three, and this for two days only. On 27 days there were a few on light duty, but the number only exceeded four on one occasion. Medical opinion was that personnel could hardly have been fitter.

The women were then moved to a searchlight site to put their training into operation. The first time they exposed their lights on a friendly 'plane there was the usual attack of nerves which happens on these occasions. It is worth noting that the lack of success on the first two night runs had a marked depressing effect. But when, on the tenth night run, operational efficiency was suddenly and rather unexpectedly reached, they were greatly pleased.

The Station was manned for the engagement of enemy aircraft on 18 nights. Enemy aircraft were only engaged twice. There was no result on either night, because the first was early in their training and the second time conditions were not favourable. But the detachment was calm in action, and this calmness was again observed when enemy aircraft were observed machine-gunning a neighbouring site. On four occasions during the experimental period the exposed a homing beacon, and as a result of one of them an aircraft was saved. Maintenance was better than expected. Here is an extract from an inspecting officer's report: -

- Generator very clean and serviceable.
- Every item serviceable.
- Lubrication and cleanliness excellent.
- Running test excellent.
- All records up-to-date and well maintained.

General remarks:

"This generator is one of the cleanest yet inspected. It is well maintained, easy to start, and obviously the pride of the troop. It is important to note that this generator is maintained and operated solely by A.T.S. personnel, and it is indeed a credit to them."

The A.T.S. also went in for field engineering, filling and laying sandbags, digging and revetting emplacements. They renovated and reconstructed field works on a derelict searchlight site which was soon to be reoccupied. The work involved shifting several tons of earth, revetting and path-making. By their tenacity of purpose they worked much faster than men and it was particularly observed that they felt no undue fatigue or ill-effects of any sort.

They did guard duty, at first working in pairs by night, but soon getting used to being alone. The tour of duty of sentries was two hours. They were armed with a pick helve, and their main duties were to challenge visitors to the site; to watch the sky for enemy aircraft and report them; to report friendly aircraft in distress, and any flares seen; to log all aircraft flying in the neighbourhood. Spirits were low at first when the results of their work were not very obvious and when it was suggested that they could not stand the winter. Spirits were highest when it was realised that the scheme was a success.

CHAPTER 23

WHAT THE GUNS REALLY DO

I N THE first two years of the war, as already stated, AA guns were responsible for destroying nearly 600 enemy aircraft over this country. Many more were damaged by AA fire, and of these a fair proportion failed to reach their home bases. This is not purely conjecture, but inference from a number of factors, such as the condition of damaged aircraft when last seen and the examination of wreckage and bodies washed ashore.

But the principal achievements of AA guns - and this is not generally realised - lie not in the destruction of enemy aircraft, in which there successes, though substantial, are bound to be few compared with the successes of fighter aircraft. The value of the guns is in the prevention of accurate bombing and in preventing enemy aircraft reaching their objectives, particularly by night. The effect of AA gunfire is generally speaking, to keep all enemy aircraft at a high altitude and to deter them from flying on the straight and even course necessary for accurate bombing. If a 'plane cannot fly low or straight, it cannot bomb accurately and its chances of doing serious damage are less. Moreover, on many occasions when A.A, guns have been heavily in action by night, particularly in the London area, 50 per cent, or more of the enemy raiders have turned back before entering the defended area, and many of the raiders which have ventured to enter it have turned back almost at once.

The direct destruction of enemy aircraft is the most obvious purpose of anti-aircraft guns, but this job is much easier for the fighters. For, to bring about the destruction of a 'plane with antiaircraft fire, the shell must burst within 50 to 100 feet from the target. With light anti-aircraft guns you must hit either the pilot, the engine or the control; and the fact that an aircraft can suffer a surprising amount of damage in other parts of its structure without being put out of action has been proved by the experiences of our own pilots in action over enemy territory. Even if the shot is perfectly aimed and the fuse is accurately set to burst the shell at exactly the right place and moment, the aircraft only has to deviate from its course to a small extent to escape unharmed.

On the other hand, unless he is using dive-bombing methods, the pilot must fly on a straight and even course at a constant speed for at least half a minute if he is to drop his bombs accurately. When the aircraft is being engaged by anti-aircraft guns the pilot has to decide whether to continue to fly straight, in which case he runs a serious risk of being hit. If, on the other hand, he "jinks" and takes avoiding action by altering his course and speed, then he ruins his bomb-aimer's chance of releasing his bombs accurately.

Another important function of AA guns is to indicate the position of enemy aircraft to our own fighters. Often, when an enemy 'plane is out of range, the guns fire one or two rounds to burst as near as possible, simply to draw the fighter's attention to the enemy.

In the nature of things, guns are bound to play second fiddle to the fighters. They have to perform the relatively humdrum job of breaking up large formations of enemy bombers so that the fighters can get in among them, and then put up with the frustration of not being allowed to fire because our own fighters are overhead.

AA work is teamwork in the highest sense of the word. The wing-forwards, who are the AA guns, do their job if they manoeuvre the ball into the right place for the centre forward - the fighter aircraft - to kick a goal.

GUNS AND GUNS POSITIONS

There are two main types of heavy AA gun. The 4.5 inch, which hurls a high explosive shell weighing nearly half a hundredweight to a height of eight miles in 50 seconds' time; and the 3.7 inch, which has almost as high a ceiling and a faster rate of fire, but a smaller shell. There are also some 3-inch guns from the last war, whose chief characteristic is a high rate of fire; these fire high explosive or shrapnel shell every three seconds, producing a mushroom growth of cotton-wool bursts.

Our light AA gun is the Bofors, which weighs two tons and fires anything up to 120 two-pound shells a minute to a height of 6,000 feet. The shell bursts on impact.

The last-war Lewis gun has been surprisingly successful, mounted singly, or in twin or quadruple for greater firepower. It has brought down many low-flying raiders who sought by diving from cloud to surprise the defences. The function of the light guns is to hold off the bomber from low-level attack, or from vulnerable points all over the country.

At a "heavy" site there may be two, four, six or eight guns. The normal plan is a four-gun site run by a half-battery divided into two sections. The two sites may be several miles from each other. Suppose a site has been chosen for a new gun position. A point in the middle has been selected from which measurements can be taken to provide accurate data for the guns and instruments when they arrive. This point is indicated, perhaps, by a cross-marked on wood bedded in concrete: it becomes the pivot of the gun-site later on. The distance and bearing from this cross to some prominent landmark is established with great accuracy by surveyors and the information is ready for the new Battery when it arrives. Other things are waiting for the Battery, too: a water-supply, which may quite likely consist of one pipe with a tap; a semi-permanent hut for the Battery office - or it may only be a marquee; some kind of shed for the cook-house; and tents or huts for messing and sleeping. There will also be a way into the site - perhaps railway sleepers thrown across a ditch at a point where a gap has been made in the hedge.

These may be the only obvious signs of preparation visible to the new Battery when it arrives; but, in fact, the selection of the site itself has involved a good deal of work. The reconnaissance of sites is a job in itself; its principles apply equally to a permanent site, such as the one that is being described, or to a position occupied temporarily by a mobile Battery. In an action of rapid movement AA defences must constantly be shifted; and in choosing successive positions a mobile Battery must apply, so far as it can, general principles. A gun position should, if possible, have an all-round field of fire with no obstruction higher than 10 degrees above ground level. If, for example, one boundary of the site is screened by tall it would be impossible to see a hostile plane approaching from that direction until it was almost on top of the guns. The gun position should also allow for effective ground defence: machine-gun posts in particular will have to be chosen to defend the gun site should it be attacked from any quarter. There must be suitable approaches and exits. It may be necessary to remove guns at a moment's notice, and if towing vehicles cannot approach easily much time will be lost. Precautions will have to be taken against sabotage. Level ground is needed for the guns

An anti-aircraft gun battery. The 4.5-inch was one of two medium anti-aircraft guns used by the Royal Artillery during the Battle.

to stand on. Administrative conveniences have to be considered - proximity of water, telephone, and electricity services. There should be as much cover as possible to make the site inconspicuous from the air; the ideal gun position will permit the disposition of living quarters, whether tents or huts, in such a way that they do not draw attention to themselves.

When the convoy arrives the Gunners see nothing but a lonely field with a few huts or tents clinging to the hedge-side. Kit is unloaded, men are detailed to their living quarters, and there is a vague promise of food as soon as the trench fire will boil the dixies.

By next morning the Battery discovers that it can eat, sleep, wash and survive even though it has been plonked down in the middle of a field "miles from anywhere" - that is to say about a mile from the nearest bus stop. And in an extraordinarily short time reconnaissance parties will have thrust round the district and come back to camp reporting amenities within striking distance.

The site has to be improved at once: tracks must be made, as inconspicuous as possible; rubble and stores unloaded; and, most important of all, the gun position has to be laid out, for the guns and instruments may arrive at any moment and the first, most urgent duty, is to report the guns "ready for action" in the shortest possible time after they arrive at the site. Among the preliminary activities are the setting up of a shelter of some sort at the gun position to accommodate personnel who will have to man the operational telephones and plotting devices. It will also be necessary to lay the operational lines from the point where the Signals have brought them to the point chosen for the shelter: this shelter is, perhaps, a tent, which later will be replaced by a hut, and in time by a sunken concrete cabin.

The guns are spaced around the sides of the gun park, with the command post at the centre. The command post is an oblong enclosure containing the predictor, the identification (or spotters) telescope, and the height-finder. It is in the charge of the Gun

Position Officer (G.P.O.) who controls the firing of the guns, watched the effect of fire, and has the responsibility of identifying any doubtful 'planes that may be about. He has an assistant - usual] an N.C.O., hereinafter referred to as G.P.O.A. - who acts as human megaphone, relaying the G.P.O.'s orders to the guns: in action the G.P.O.A. is responsible for "fire discipline," for seeing that the correct drill is followed and no unnecessary risks .ire run. Well-given orders make an extraordinary difference to the number! of rounds the guns manage to fire.

An approaching 'plane is first seen through the spotter's telescope a simple affair with two eye-pieces, which looks quite unlike a telescope. If it is a friendly 'plane, the spotter logs it in a book; if it is hostile, he sounds the alarm. The trouble starts when he mis-identifies a hostile 'plane as friendly. But spotters are uncannily) skilled and their appropriate senses are inhumanly specialised.

They are not usually enthusiastic to take on the job, but they quickly develop the specialist's sense of superiority and supplement their official handbooks with privately purchased textbooks.

Once the spotter is on the target the G.P.O.A. shouts to everybody else the height and bearing which he reads from scales at the base of the telescope. To do this he must stoop, and, unless he is nimble, he may block the spotter's view. Then the spotter roars out, "Telescope! Telescope!" and the G.P.O.A. tries to dodge out of the way without losing sight of the height and bearing scales. It is not enough to announce where the 'plane was when first seen. The spotter has to keep his telescope on the target as it moves, and, in order to overcome the time-lag between shouting out heights and bearings, and the flight of the 'plane, the G.P.O.A. must estimate ahead: when he is skilful he does not read out the height and bearing registered on the scales, but makes adjustments so that when the predictor and height-finder are registering the figures he shouts, the target will be within their field of view. It is a breathless and exciting business. The G.P.O.A.'s voice is relentless:

"Bearing 154! Angle 20" ("Angle" means "angle of elevation".)

"Bearing 158! Angle 20!"

Then comes the report:

"Predictor on target"

"Height-finder on target"

When the G.P.O.A. has heard both these reports, and not before, he tells the G.P.O., "Section on target," and the Battery is ready to make the best use of any information which the predictor may provide.

The heart of the command post is the predictor - the calculating machine that finds out where a 'plane is and predicts its future movements, so that allowances can be made in laying aim. Its calculations are based on information provided partly by the layers and partly by the height-finder, which can tell not only the height of the 'plane but its distance from the gun she.

The findings of the predictor are transmitted to the guns by pointers on dials - two dials for each gun, one recording bearing and one elevation. Gunners, who watch these dials, follow the pointer with another pointer, and by this means swing the gun round and move it up or down according to the readings from the predictor.

In addition to all this activity on ground level, much is done in a shelter probably sunk some way in the ground. This room is the link which every gun position has with the vast system of the Royal Observer Corps and other sources of information. The connection is not, of course, direct; but the operational line from a central control room in the gun defence area supplies news of the movement of aircraft which is often gathered in the first place from the Royal Observer Corps.

Two telephonists write down and transmit messages between the command post and the gun operations room. This is a trying job, with long hours when nothing is happening: then a lot begins to happen at once; and if one miscounts the pips it means a wrong plot being made, and perhaps a target being missed.

The G.P.O. and G.P.O.A., standing in the Command Post, can see into the gun-pits. This, too, is essential, because the men in charge of the various gun detachments - the "Numbers 1" - must acknowledge all orders from the Command Post. By day they shoot an arm straight up; by night, they use the word "Through!" The importance of acknowledgment cannot be fully realised except during the height of an action, when the noise is deafening and the gun detachments have only one thought - to send up more rounds. As a rule, each detachment has its own gun which it tends and cherishes with personal affection: this is not surprising, for the gun itself is a graceful and lovely instrument. Perhaps that is why gun crews nearly always give their guns feminine names. This personal affection owes something to the fact that the crews have to build the pit for their gun, and have much the same anxious pride in the task as the dresser of a famous or aspiring actress has in getting her charge ready for a sensational part.

This is how the gunners "make up" their gun. The gun arrives and is levelled. Round it the pit is dug with its half a dozen recesses. The walls gradually rise and arc camouflaged, strengthened with sandbags and covered with turf. The recesses are use partly for the storage of ammunition. This has to be stacked with great care. Long, metal boxes, each containing two rounds of ammunition, are stored in such a way that air can circulate all round: no two boxes should touch. Strips of wood separate the layers of ammunition boxes. All the rounds are regularly examined every day to guard against damage by rust or condensation. One recess is reserved for the Limber Gunner. There should be a strong wooden bench in it so that he can dismantle and clean the breech mechanism. Another recess is used as a shelter. During long night alerts there are many periods when the men cannot leave the gun park, but there is no need for them to be at their positions on the gun. They go to their shelter and sit there in the darkness huddled together and half dozing, but with an car cocked for "Take Post"; and when the order comes from the Command Post they have to be back at their positions on the gun in a matter of seconds.

Normally a gunner has one day off per week and one evening. Why is there so little time to spare?

There are only two guns per section and only eleven men are needed for each gun team. But apart from the fact, which the outside world finds so difficult to grasp, that when you say you have such and such a number of men on the strength you don't really mean it because most of them are always doing something else, there are various other commitments to be considered.

Take the case of a half-battery, with a nominal roll of, say, 140 men. Ready for action at any minute of every day and night you must have 44 men for the four guns. There must be six to eight men working the predictor and three or four the height-finder. There is a fire picquet, a decontamination squad, stretcher-bearers, a medical orderly and a guard. Five men are away on courses at divisional and brigade schools. Six are away from camp ding a temporarily unoccupied gun site five miles away. One of the cooks has been commandeered by brigade headquarters. Six men are in hospital and six are sick in camp. Fifteen men are on seven days' leave. Twenty men are having their weekly day off. That is why only eleven men can go out this evening. Incidentally, while they are manning the guns or acting as fire picquet, they are kept busy all day with training, with maintenance of their equipment, with P.T., with arms drill, and above all with fatigues and construction work on the camp. There is plenty to do in keeping them up to scratch in all their obligations and duties. For without the incentive of enemy 'planes to shoot at, efficiency is liable to decline quickly. There is always plenty to do except when it rains. But it is not a life of all work and no play. Here is a scene which often occurs in every fixed station.

The battery canteen has been transformed into a concert hall. A stage has been rigged up at one end with some rather insecure-looking curtains. The officers sit on chairs in the first few rows;

the men are packed crouch-backed on forms behind. An orchestra of seven is packed at the foot of the stage. Its members keep disappearing, for they provide the bulk of the stage show.

At the moment, the battery sergeant major and the battery quartermaster-sergeant are doing a cross-talk act which is supposed to be a scene between a sergeant and a new recruit.

What's your trade in civilian life?

Spotter, chum.

Don't call me chum. Call me sergeant.

What! Don't you like being called chum, chum?

Right, we'll try a bit of rifle drill. Now what we're going on with this morning is slope arms by numbers. Slope arms by numbers - one. That's good. Two. Three. Why, you've been in the army before.

No, never, sergeant.

Well, where did you learn that rifle drill?

I was three years in the chorus of Desert Song.

All these shows tend to fall into a generic shape, based on a rather gangling orchestra of about six - piano, drums, piano accordion, saxophone, guitar, possibly a trumpet and a violin. The leader is probably a professional or semi-professional musician of good or fair ability, whose energy is responsible for the organisation of the band. They are almost bound to play "Tiger R."

There is likely to be a male voice choir whose choice of music is often strange, ranging from little-known highbrow works to "Oh, who will o'er the Downs so free."

The solo violinist, another fundamental, is more handicapped than the baritone and the tenor by the faulty tuning of the piano. There is the man who does animal impressions, and the man who impersonates Lionel Barrymore and Ned Sparks. There is an occasional freak act. One man eats two lamp bulbs; an ashtray, tour safety razor blades and a gramophone record, finishing up with a few lighted cigarettes - all with apparent relish and no ill effects.

Somewhere in the Command there is a professional escapologist-a fine act. But good "freaks" are as rare as the piano accordionist is common. The piano accordionist is the backbone of most concert parties: his appeal never fails.

Besides the Battery concert parties there are constituted and recognized Brigade Concert Parties such as "The Blue Pencils" and "The Moon and Stars" who do a full time job and make substantial sums of for Army Welfare and regimental funds. Some Regimental Commanding Officers have formed small concert parties, which tour the sites, usually on a part-time basis. These little concert parties do a lot of good, penetrating where nothing much else does.

Concert parties are officially encourages by A.A. Command, which has a hierarchy of entertainment officers whose job consists largely in getting things going. Most officers realise the value of entertainment, especially good home-made entertainment, as an ingredient of morale: but there are few Commanders who believe that entertainment is either unnecessary or actively detrimental: though, in fact, far from taking men's minds off their job, it freshens them by its contrast value.

In addition to these concert parties there is the wireless - notably the special programme broadcast twice a week and known as "Ack- Ack, Beer- Beer" edited by Bill Mclurg. Usually about 40 men and woman take part in the programme; 50 per cent of the actual entertainers are professional or semi-professional in civilian life.

- C H A P T E R   2 4 -

BALLOONS IN BATTLE

A T TEN minutes to nine on the fine morning of the last day of August 1940, the Germans gave a clear indication of their respect for the British balloon barrage - in their own language. They came across to Dover and shot down every one of the twenty-three balloons flying there in six minutes.

The Battle of Britain had been joined; and the Dover balloons - which had been deployed during July as a protection against dive bombing - represented the first line of our passive defence. And they still fly in full view of the enemy; proof of his failure, by this and subsequent attacks, to force us to discontinue the Dover barrage.

The attack began when two waves of about 50 enemy aircraft approached Dover at heights of from 15,000 to 20,000 feet. Six Messerschmitt 109s broke away from these formations and flew at the balloons. This first attack was more successful than any subsequently made, but nevertheless half the force was destroyed; two aircraft were shot down by anti-aircraft fire and a third by rifle tire from balloon crews.

There were no casualties among the balloon operators, and replacements were immediately put in hand. One crew raised a new balloon within 40 minutes, by 11.30 eleven balloons were flying again over Dover, and by the same afternoon their number was increased to eighteen. At 7.30 in the evening the Germans tried again and shot fifteen more balloons down. But despite these losses, there were sixteen balloons flying over Dover on the following morning.

When these were attacked, three enemy aircraft were shot down at a cost of only two balloons. The crew of a site in the centre of the town lost their balloon but reported as follows: "The enemy aircraft attacked a balloon which was rising just inflated in the harbour. A 50-round burst of controlled rifle fire staggered the machine, which banked up, clearly disclosing underpart and markings. A second burst of 20 rounds was fired and black smoke was seen coming from the engine, and the machine dived into the sea beyond the breakwater."

Here is another report of the same occurrence. "On this particular Saturday we were clearing up in the billet when the crackle of machine and cannon guns was heard. Everyone grabbed his rifle and dashed on to the site. The sky was full of AA shell bursts white machine guns were going off everywhere. Several balloons were coming down in flames, ours included. The next balloon to us was being hauled down just as fast as the winch could pull it. It was about 800 ft. off the ground when one of the Me.109s decided that he would try and get it. He swept over our heads and got it all right. But as he turned and banked away to go out to sea again, he seemed to be standing still in the air for a few seconds.

"The range then was about 700 ft. The N.C.O. in charge yelled fire! Everyone pumped as many rounds as they could into it. The Me. kept straight on with his dive out to sea, while a thin trail of smoke poured out from behind. When we last saw it, it was going down behind the breakwater out to sea. We didn't have time to stand about wondering if we had got it as we had a new balloon to inflate and fly. This was accomplished in a very short space of time. It was when we had finished this and had the barrage up again that we learnt that we had been given the credit for shooting down a Me.109."

The protective balloons still fly over Dover. The attack on the barrage has proved too costly. Subsequent attacks appear to represent individual acts of daring by members of the *Luftwaffe* and are said to be frowned upon by the German authorities. The enemy has been convinced that the game is not worth the candle. The however, that be tried these attacks shows his high opinion of their value and confirmation of this is provided by a special correspondent of the Giornale a'Italia, Carlo d'Ongaro, writing

Putting the balloons to bed in giant hangars is part of the intensive training undertaken by balloon operators.

from the north coast of France about a raid on Filton carried out by Ober-Leutnant Hollinde.

"This was one of the most difficult raids carried out by the *Luftwaffe* on England, on account of the exceptional defences at the Filton Works designed to keep off dive bombers. Two rows of balloons were placed round the installations like two concentric circles, and each balloon was very close to the next. They were flying at a height of over 1,200 metres, and their diameter was such that they formed a sort of well into which no pilot in his senses would think of going. Ober-Leutnant Hollinde was aware of the difficulties and for several days he practiced aerobatics and worked out the best method of attack. Finally he selected a suitable day with bands of clouds moving across the sky. The buildings at Filton are camouflaged and not easily identified, but the balloon barrage was clearly visible and was useful for locating the target.

"Hollinde dived down vertically from 3,000 metres and released all the bombs he was carrying: but, although the entry into the balloon well was a practically normal manoeuvre for a pilot of his class, entailing only courage and skill, to get out again was another matter. In view of the speed of his aircraft he could not keep on a straight course inside the balloons, and. circling round, he tried to gain height. He was flying so low that he could see the faces of the AA gunners, and his gunner fired on the gun crews and on the balloons in turn, but his fire was not sufficient either to silence the guns or to open a was through the balloons. Hollinde then decided to try a dangerous manoeuvre and he went into a sideslip and slipped between the balloon cables. Even then he was only inside the second circle, where the balloons were still closer, but he had no time to waste as the daylight was going and he would not have been able to see the cables. Fortunately for him his manoeuvre again succeeded and he returned safely to base."

Finally, William Shirer's Berlin Diary records the attitude of German pilots toward the London barrage. "He (one of the German pilots) relates that they approached London at a height of from 15/16,000 feet, dived to about 10,000 feet and released their bombs at this height - too high for accurate night bombing. They did not dare to go below 7,000 feet, he says, on account of the barrage balloons."

These two examples of the enemy's opinion of the balloon barrage illustrate its primary object which is to drive the enemy to a height from which accurate bombing is difficult rather than to net him. They indicate too that the barrage is successful either in driving the enemy up or in making him alter his course and disturbing his aim. A report from the Commanding Officer of a naval vessel written in January 1941 stresses the value of balloons in upsetting the aim of attacking bombers.

"At 10.45 hours on December 27th, while steaming northwards off the North-east Spit Buoy, my ship was attacked by two enemy aircraft. The first bombing attack was turned, apparently by a rather late appreciation of the presence of the balloon barrage, necessitating a sudden swerve on the part of the airmen; no bombs were dropped.

Repeating the attack again from stern, two bombs were dropped about half a cable off my port quarter and it is considered that the balloon prevented a closer attack."

Apart from attempts at shooting them down the Germans have shown their respect for the balloon barrage in another way. Balloon fenders have been found upon enemy aircraft brought down in this country. This fender is a guard stretching from each wing tip to the nose, and consists of a streamlined shell of light alloy reinforced with a strip of steel along the leading edge, forming a sort of flattened V in front of the aircraft, held in position by five outrigger struts. It is intended that this fender should be strong enough to break the balloon cables by impact or to thrust them aside; but it weighs about 800 lbs. and reduces the performance of the aircraft very considerably.

Moreover, the fact that enemy bombers are forced to fly high over their targets reduces their chances of avoiding our own fighters en route until some experience had been gained of the working of the barrage in the Metropolis.

A ring of balloons flying at a radius of about seven and a half miles from Charing Cross was first envisaged as a layout for the London barrage. The balloons were to be spaced ten to a mile, giving a total of 450 balloons at approximately 200-yard intervals. The stockade idea had been abandoned. The new barrage was conceived as flexible, each balloon being independent and mobile.

To this end a preliminary survey of the 45-mile circle round London was undertaken. Hut almost before it had started the idea of "perimeter siting" was abandoned in favour of "field siting." Balloons dotted all over a protected area would, obviously, force an attacking aircraft lo fly above them all the time. If, however, the original idea had been carried out the aircraft need only have flown over the protecting screen when it would have been able to come in as low as it liked to make its attack.

At this stage the question of operational height had to be considered. A balloon has to lift not only its own weight but also the weight of its cable. The higher a balloon is to fly, therefore, the greater must be its volume to give it lifting capacity. No doubt the ideal would be to fly balloons at such a height that enemy aircraft could never fly over them, but this would mean a balloon so large that it would be extremely difficult to handle on the ground, particularly in a built-up area. It was therefore decided to operate balloons at medium heights, preventing accurate aiming and dive-bombing and at the same time leaving the upper air free for fighter interception.

It would have been uneconomical in peacetime to maintain a permanent strength of operators for the full London barrage. Moreover, the presence of so many balloons in and around London would have been too great a menace to peacetime air traffic. An auxiliary organisation on the same lines as that of the Territorial army was therefore, introduced.

The Balloon Squadrons were to be manned principally by

auxiliarie able to do part-time or week-end training in association with a small nucleus of regular personnel and concentrated in four main depots in the metropolitan area to be defended. These centres were the first meeting grounds of the many who volunteered their services and who still maintain protective barrages throughout the country at the present day. They were used both as storage depots and for training the squadrons which would be deployed to their own war sites in the event of war. Today the centres are used as maintenance and supply depots for squadrons in the field.

The majority of the balloons for use in war were stored and packed in these centres, a small number being kept inflated for training and test purposes. The selection of suitable positions for the centres in the crowded environs of London presented great difficulty in itself. An area of up to 80 acres was required, situated within reasonable distance of the war sites, accessible for auxiliaries travelling from their homes in spare time, and not too close to existing airfields to interfere with flying.

The convoy flies its protective barrage. These balloons manned by R.A.F. crews offer a serious obstacle to the dive bomber. They are smaller and easier to handle than those of our land defenses.

Early in 1938 work was started, and the recruiting of the first balloon squadrons commenced. A balloon training school was opened, and a nucleus of regular personnel was given an intensive course of training before being posted to the various centres. A balloon group headquarters under Fighter Command was also formed to control and administer the barrage as a whole and Air Commodore J. G. Hearson took up his appointment as the first Air Officer Commanding.

At the time of the international crisis in September 1938 the organisation was sufficiently developed to permit a partial mobilisation of the barrage and some squadrons were deployed fully equipped to their war sites. They remained on a war footing for about ten days, but were eventually withdrawn after a useful exercise had been carried out.

The performance of the London barrage units had, indeed, been so satisfactory that it was decided to proceed with the establishment of barrages in many of the important provincial cities. The first to be chosen were Portsmouth, Southampton, Plymouth, Bristol. Cardiff, Swansea, Liverpool, Manchester, Glasgow, Newcastle. Sheffield, Hull, Birmingham and Coventry. And with this expansion came the decision to establish a separate Balloon Command.

Early in 1939 the provincial groups were established on a skeleton basis, and sufficient progress had been made by September to enable the barrage for the whole country to be mobilised.

WHEN THE BALLOON GOES UP

At the outbreak of war a small group assembled on the roof of the Air Ministry in Whitehall to watch the first wartime barrage make its appearance. Punctually to the minute it rose into the clear autumn skies. At once logical and preposterous, comforting and extraordinary, these first balloons were made welcome as a new aspect of city life. Throughout the length and breadth of the country their crews and the public hastened to christen them. Within three days of the beginning of war, a balloon flying above an archbishop's palace was locally known as the 'Archblimp.' More often a feminine name was regarded for some reason as appropriate. The balloon and its successors at the Dover site whose crew shot down the Messerschmitt with their rifles are called 'Matilda.' The advent of W.A.A.F. balloon crews recently started a more romantic fashion in names. The first W.A.A.F. crew to operate in London christened their charge 'Romeo.'

The balloon barrage is nowadays so familiar that we tend to take it for granted. In fact its maintenance calls for the exercise of much individual skill and for much organisation behind the scenes.

The usual type of barrage balloon is a streamlined bag of rubber-proofed cotton fabric, specially treated, with a gas capacity of 19,150 cubic feet, a length overall of about 63 feet, and a height of just over 31 feet. It weighs approximately 550 lbs. and it is flown on a flexible steel cable. On the outbreak of war it took at least 40 minutes for any single balloon to rise into the air; it now takes less than 20 minutes. Such is the progress achieved in a new and by no means easy technique.

Balloons rise because they are filled with hydrogen which is many times lighter than air. Now if 1 cubic foot of hydrogen gas rises, the ever diminishing atmospheric pressure will cause it to expand. In fact if it reached a height of 19,000 feet it would expand to 2 cubic feet. Increases in temperature also cause expansion. Allowance must therefore be made for gas expansion at operational flying levels.

The French made their balloons with elastic sides, but this did not work well in practice. The envelopes of British balloons have false bottoms filled with air which is expelled as soon as the gas chamber expands. This 'false bottom' is known as the ballonct, and the flexible wall which separates it from the gas chamber is the diaphragm. When a balloon is inflated at ground level, the upper compartment is not filled to capacity with gas and the ballonet is filled with air through its wind scoop. The balloon goes up, the atmospheric pressure decreases, and the expanding gas presses the air out of the ballonet. As the balloon descends, the ballonet scoops back air when the gas contracts. So the shape of the balloon remains constant and the three air-inflated stabilizers, like two huge fins and a rudder, enable the balloon to ride head-to-wind always on an even keel.

These are the rudiments of a barrage balloon. But there is a highly specialised and constantly improving technique in flight - manipulation, close-hauling, bedding down, and always, day and night, getting the best of the weather.

At the outbreak of war all balloons were flown directly from the leading-off gear at the back of their winches, all of which were motorised. To moor the balloon on the ground it was necessary to peg out a wire bed and manually to haul the balloon down, after it had been brought to within a few yards of the ground, by means of handling guys and a rope tackle.

With every change of wind the balloon had to be let up from its bed into its flying position while the bed was re-laid, because it is essential to keep a balloon head to wind. This was often impossible in turbulent weather, particularly at night and the only alternative was to leave the balloon broadside to the wind and pray for the dawn. In November 1939, this resulted in a 50 per cent, casualty rate throughout the entire barrage.

Such a problem had never arisen before. Observation balloon operators in the past could choose their sites and their weather. The new barrage principle of field siting allowed no such power of selection. Clearly an all-directional bed was necessary upon which a balloon could be turned in all weathers without releasing its moorings or moving the winch.

The answer was a homely millstone purchased for a few pence from a Borough Council yard. It was pushed through Hampstead by a balloon crew and rolled on to the sacrosanct turf of Hampstead Cricket Club. Almost between the creases a pit was dug, into which the millstone was rolled with a chain reeved through it. The hole was filled up and the turf replaced, leaving only a few links of the chain above ground to which an ordinary cable pulley was attached. From this pulley the balloon was actually flown, and the winch was withdrawn to an onlooker's position at the side of the ground. The all-directional bed where the balloon could be safely moored in all weathers and kept head to wind was provided by a rope or wire cradle and wire mooring circle now generally used throughout Great Britain.

The rope cradle consists of 12 rope legs attached to the central anchorage. The ends of these legs are loaded with sandbags, to which the balloon is attached by means of tensioning slips. When the balloon is to be turned, the rope cradle and bags are dragged round by hand, and the handling guys and picketing lines by which the balloon is moored are stepped round one at a time in the direction which the balloon is to follow. In this manner the

A depot barge of the Kite Balloon Section, sea-going balloons were at one time painted in a diced pattern for camouflage purposes.

balloon can be turned without running the many risks of releasing it from its bed. The familiar array of sandbags on balloon sites was replaced later by concrete ballast blocks which are easier to handle, are neater and last a lot longer.

A more recent improvement is the tail-guy mooring which enables the balloon to be moored with its stabilizers filled with air ready to be raised at a moment's notice. This achieves a state of readiness throughout the barrage which is of the greatest operational importance. It enables the balloon, without resort to the use of handling guys, to be held at two points only - by the flying rigging at the point of attachment and at the stern of the balloon itself by the tail guy. The tail guy is attached to a wire circle about 180 feet in diameter, and it is simply shifted along the perimeter wire when it is desired to turn the balloon head to wind.

In tolerable weather balloons can be left flying on the tail-guy mooring, and several minutes can be saved in raising each balloon into the air: but in really turbulent weather they are better bedded down.

Amid the vagaries of the British climate the flying of thousands of balloons presents an hourly struggle with the weather. One of the greatest potential dangers is lightning. At four o'clock on an afternoon in February 1939, only two flashes of lightning were recorded in the whole of Great Britain. But one destroyed a balloon at Stanmore, the other a balloon at Chigwell. Captive balloons, attached as they are to the end of a metal cable which forms in itself an efficient lightning conductor, were found, in fact, to be very vulnerable to lightning if flown during thunderstorms; and, as hydrogen is a highly inflammable gas they don't last long if they are struck.

During the autumn of 1939 as many as 80 balloons were burned in the air in one afternoon in London alone. Arrangements were therefore made for weather forecasts of thundery conditions to be supplied throughout Balloon Command, and as many balloons as possible are now bedded down when there is danger of lightning.

In view of the very localised nature of thunderstorms this policy would, if followed rigidly, result in unnecessary curtailment of flying. Moreover the tactical situation at times may demand that balloons should be flown in thunderstorms. It was, therefore, essential for lightning protection to be provided, and widespread investigations were undertaken, in the course of which balloon crews themselves gave valuable help in handling the scientific instruments used.

As a result a practical form of lightning protection has been devised which, whilst not giving complete immunity, does minimise the risk. The results of the experiments also led to the construction of an instrument which uses any electrical currents flowing in the balloon cable to give warning of the approach of highly dangerous conditions. When in fact a balloon is struck by lightning, the electricity passes to earth through the winch or anchorage from which the balloon is flown. Members of a crew near the foot of the cable therefore have to take precautions, and these have been designed and thoroughly tested on the largest electrical discharges which can be artificially produced. Amongst the precautions which are now routine practice on all sites, is that of always jumping on to or off a winch in order to avoid conducting a discharge. This and other precautions minimise a very real danger to balloon crews.

THE CREWS THAT MAN THEM

A balloon crew originally consisted of two corporals and ten men; but progress in balloon manipulation has made it possible to reduce the crew to two corporals and eight men. These numbers allow for leave, sickness and absence on courses and in practice a corporal and five airmen can manage a balloon satisfactorily. The necessity for maintaining a constant guard by day and night takes up much of their time, however, and makes it impossible to reduce the size of the crew.

In spite of the fact that the speed of operation has been enormously increased, the physical labour entailed in manipulation has decreased in many ways. In early days the public was familiar with the sight of a balloon crew hauling the balloon down from ten yards or so off the ground to its bed by means of a rope tackle. This operation is now carried out by means of a windlass on the side of the winch, and in many other ways manual work has been eliminated

Nevertheless a balloon crew has an exceedingly full day, as is illustrated by the words of a balloon operator in the centre of London:

"'Come on - ten to two!' With these few choice words I find myself rudely awakened from my warm blanket bed to go on Guard for two hours. Having completed this duty and being relieved, I crawl back to bed and attempt to get a three hours' sleep. At 07.00 hours the Mess Orderly for the day awakens me along with the remainder of the Crew, to commence our many varied duties of the day. After breakfast, having done my share of cleaning the billet, personal equipment and rifle, I proceed to Flight Headquarters to collect three thousand bricks to bring back and unload on my site, where the remainder of the Crew are digging up the turf lo a depth of six inches and laying a brick bed.

I make my way back to the site in time for tea (16.30 hours). After a much-needed wash, I proceed to look at the Guard List (the ever-present duty) finding myself 'fixed' for two hours from 22.00 hrs. to 23.59 hrs. This regular happening is unavoidable. After cleaning myself up I make my bed and take the opportunity of an hour or two of leisure before my Guard. At 22.30 hours I report to the Visiting Duty Officer, and at 23.45 hrs. just as I am preparing to be relieved after a last walk round the site, an Operational broadcast is received giving an order to bed down the balloon, due to bad weather. I turn the Crew out and finally, after completing this operation, I retire to my much-needed bed."

The W.A.A.F. takes over. The handling of barrage balloons requires skill, teamwork and considerable physical strength

DAILY ROUTINE DUTIES

They don't have to deal with three thousand bricks every day but, apart from this, they have obviously plenty to do. Much time is spent on maintenance. The daily routine duties carried out on a site include the following:

Operational orders to fly, alter height, close-haul or bed the balloon. Switch on or off Rip Link.

Daily Inspections.

Keeping Balloon head to wind on the bed, Tail Guy Mooring or Interim Close-haul.

Maintenance of Balloon: Repairs and Topping-up.

Maintenance of Wince: Cleaning and Brake tests. Winch Tool Maintenance and Check.

Maintenance of Bed: Blocks, Tackle, Bedwires, Pyramid, Cradle, Sandbags, Slips, Ragbolts, "U-bolts. Ringbolts, Screw pickets, 90-foot Circle and Strops, Tail Guy Snatchblock, Central Anchorage Snatchblock.

Maintenance of Flying Cable: Oil and inspect throughout.

Inspection and Maintenance of Armaments.

- Gas Drill.
- Defence and Weapon Training.
- Lay-out of Kits and Bedding.
- Maintenance and Cleaning of Personal Kit.
- Messing Fatigues and Site Cooking.
- Inspection and Maintenance of Gas Cylinders, Trailer, Topping-up and Inflation Equipment.

Balloon crews were accommodated in the early days in tents and fed on rations supplied in hay boxes from central kitchens. Accommodation is now usually in hutments: to an increasing extent food is cooked on the spot.

The following account from one of the auxiliaries who took

part in the first deployment of the provincial barrages recalls the atmosphere of those first days of war.

"War declared - fly all balloons, and the sixteen balloons of two flights of the first squadron of Manchester rose as one, simultaneously with London. The billets here, there and everywhere, improvised, cajoled, demanded. High-hat houses, mean houses, factory floors - no blankets, no huts, no tents, nothing. Millions of children and thousands of irate ladies indicating that they could not feed and house 12 lusty men for ever for nothing. But the balloons flew - came down somehow, and went up somehow. Improvise, manage, do without, get hot, get cold, get hungry, stay hungry, Office work started, telephones used at the local grocer's, Flight H.Q. in the local pub, provided with piles of pennies for calls. But the balloons flew, and more balloons. The auxiliaries who stuck all this with us were mostly not young. The butcher, baker, banker - all did their damnedest."

In the middle of January 1941, the Air Officer Commanding, Balloon Command, was asked to consider a suggestion that the flying of balloons could be completely carried out by the W.A.A.F. At first this suggestion was received with some dismay. The fact that the manning of balloons for 24 hours a day, frequently in the most appalling weather conditions, required physical strength not generally possessed by women, was considered in itself sufficient reason for rejecting it.

Nevertheless, the Air Officer Commanding examined the problem with the utmost care. Every aspect of the suggestion was explored, from the physical suitability of women as balloon operators to the accommodation that they would require; from the amount of food to be issued to them to the type of clothes they would have to wear; from the strength of W.A.A.F. crews to the question of whether or not they should use lethal weapons. After a great deal of thought an experiment was finally made to see just what the airwomen of the W.A.A.F. could, or could not, do when they got on to a balloon site.

Thus one cold, wet morning in April 1941, 20 W.A.A.F. Balloon Fabric workers, all volunteers, dressed in oilskins and sou'westers, marched on to a training site at a balloon centre just outside London. There, under the guidance of eight R.A.F. balloon operators, and watched by a group of senior R.A.F. technical and medical officers, they carried out a number of simple balloon operations for the first time. The experiment, like the rain, lasted all day. But at the end of it the W.A.A.F. emerged successfully.

A month later the first batch of W.A.A.F. - again all volunteers and mostly balloon-fabric workers - were posted to the largest balloon training centre in the country for ten weeks intensive training. At the end of the course the W.A.A.F. Balloon Operators were once more put through their paces for the benefit of senior R.A.F. Officers.

The scene on this occasion was very different from that wet morning in April. Sun had taken the place of rain. The oilskins and sou'westers had disappeared, and in their place the airwomen wore smart air-force-blue working suits. The pale faces of yesterday were now tanned by the July sun. And most important of all, the enthusiastic but inexperienced W.A.A.F. of April were now carrying out the complicated balloon operations with all the ease and efficiency of the R.A.F.

A few days later the Air Officer Commanding was able to report to the Secretary of State for Air: "Training has proceeded to the extent that it has now been found possible to draft women to war sites in the Balloon Barrage, which sites they will in a few days time be in course of taking over from the airmen." Every week since then the W.A.A.F. have taken over more and more balloon sites. They will continue to do so until a very large proportion of the Balloon Barrages in the British Isles will be manned by airwomen, the airmen being remustered to, or trained for, more arduous jobs.

The substitution of W.A.A.F. for airmen on balloon sites does not imply that the airmen, who have operated in all weathers and under aerial bombardment, have in any sense been doing a "woman's job." In the first place, it requires a crew of 16 airwomen to replace 10 airmen. Secondly, it must be borne in mind that R.A.F. crews are incorporated in military defence schemes, whereas W.A.A.F. are not. Thus, in a number of areas it is not practicable for W.A.A.F. to take over sites.

Lastly, it is only the great progress in and simplification of balloon manipulation, for which the original officers and airmen of Balloon Command are responsible, that has made the substitution at all possible. Skill and intelligence will still be required, but the constant physical strain which was present in the past has been very much reduced.

The Balloon Operators of the W.A.A.F. will still have to endure the weather as well as attack from the air, but they have already shown that they can take it. Theirs is undoubtedly one of the hardest jobs undertaken by women in this war, but they have tackled it and succeeded at it.

GERMAN LUFTWAFFE LOSSES, JULY-SEPTEMBER 1940

Operational Aircraft Losses, Jul-Sep 1940

Aircraft Type	Operational Strength, 29 Jun 1940	Losses to Enemy Action	Other Losses	Total
Single-Engined Fighters	1,107	398	79	518
Twin-Engined Fighters	357	214	9	235
Bobmers	1,380	424	127	621
Dive Bombers	428	59	10	88

Aircraft Combat Losses by Type, 10 Jul - 11 Aug 1940

Cause	Destroyed	Damaged	Total
Bomber	72	33	105
Dive Bomber	22	20	42
Bf 109	61	23	84
Bf 110	27	17	44
Reconnaissance	18	5	23
Seaplane	16	2	18
Total	216	100	316

Aircraft and Crew Losses, Aug 1940

Aircraft Type	Aircraft Written Off	Airmen Killed	Captured	Injured	Uninjured	Missing
Bf 109	229	57	3	41	47	84
Bf 110	123	48	2	6	19	48
Do 17 Fliegender Bleistift	75	22	2	14	10	26
He 111 Doppel-Blitz	98	36	1	9	15	34
Ju 88	104	33	4	5	17	44
Ju 87 Stuka	62	20	1	5	9	28

RAF Fighter Command Casualties, Jul-Sep 1940

Date	Lost	Damaged
1-7 Jul	3 Blenheim, 1 Hurricane, 3 Spitfire	2 Hurricane
8-14 Jul	16 Hurricane, 7 Spitfire	6 Hurricane, 2 Spitfire
15-21 Jul	6 Defiant, 10 Hurricane, 6 Spitfire	5 Hurricane
22-28 Jul	4 Hurricane, 12 Spitfire	1 Hurricane, 6 Spitfire
29 Jul-4 Aug	4 Hurricane, 4 Spitfire	None
5-11 Aug	3 Blenheim (incl. 1 trainer), 33 Hurricane, 12 Spitfire	3 Hurricane, 10 Spitfire
12-18 Aug	29 Hurricane, 10 Spitfire, 76 Unidentified	5 Hurricane, 8 Spitfire
19-25 Aug	4 Defiant, 20 Hurricane, 23 Spitfire	1 Hurricane
26 Aug-1 Sep	7 Defiant, 81 Hurricane, 47 Spitfire	10 Hurricane, 6 Spitfire
2-8 Sep	4 Blenheim, 74 Hurricane, 52 Spitfire	34 Hurricane, 31 Spitfire
9-15 Sep	59 Hurricane, 28 Spitfire	20 Hurricane, 15 Spitfire
16-22 Sep	12 Hurricane, 7 Spitfire, 7 Unidentified	9 Spitfire
23-29 Sep	46 Hurricane, 32 Spitfire	23 Hurricane, 24 Spitfire

British Weekly Fighter Aircraft Production, Apr-Oct 1940

Week Ending	Beaufighter	Defiant	Hurricane	Spitfire
6 April	0	5	35	14
13 April	1	3	38	17
20 April	0	3	41	13
27 April	0	6	40	14
4 May	0	3	34	15
11 May	0	5	41	12
18 May	0	4	40	14
25 May	0	4	59	17
1 June	0	8	87	22
8 June	0	2	79	22
15 June	0	7	67	25
22 June	2	8	75	21
29 June	0	13	68	26
6 July	0	12	65	32
13 July	0	12	57	30
20 July	1	11	67	41
27 July	4	14	65	37
3 August	3	13	68	41
10 August	5	10	64	37
17 August	5	11	43	31
24 August	5	8	64	44
31 August	5	3	54	37
7 September	5	11	54	36
14 September	6	10	56	38
21 September	4	6	57	40
28 September	0	10	58	34
5 October	0	12	60	32
12 October	4	11	55	31
19 October	6	8	55	25
26 October	9	16	69	42
2 November	3	10	56	41

Aircraft Losses Between 10 Jul and 11 Aug, 1940

Cause	Destroyed	Damaged	Total
Bf 109	87	52	139
Bf 110	6	10	6
Bomber	13	38	51
Collision	4	1	5
Anti-Aircraft	1	1	2
Friendly	1	3	4
Unknown Combat	3	1	4
Non-Combat	47	68	115
Total	162	174	336

MORE FROM THE SAME SERIES

Most books from the 'World War II from Original Sources' series are edited and endorsed by Emmy Award winning film maker and military historian Bob Carruthers, producer of Discovery Channel's Line of Fire and Weapons of War and BBC's Both Sides of the Line. Long experience and strong editorial control gives the military history enthusiast the ability to buy with confidence.

The series advisor is David McWhinnie, producer of the acclaimed Battlefield series for Discovery Channel. David and Bob have co-produced books and films with a wide variety of the UK's leading historians including Professor John Erickson and Dr David Chandler.

Where possible the books draw on rare primary sources to give the military enthusiast new insights into a fascinating subject.

For more information visit www.pen-and-sword.co.uk